Win-Win Finesse

The Art of Dealing Positively
with Negative Feeling

Congratulations
Patricia & Belly Ray
on your
Happy Day 2/26/05!

Paschal Baute

Praise for Win-Win Finesse

"I wish I had this insight when I was running the manufacturing plants during my 30 working years.
—Tom McAllister, retired Plant Manager.

"A charming lesson in giving negative feedback, with deep implications for reverencing the people you work with, and caring about their feelings."
—William Cleary, author *Prayers For Lovers* and other books.

"This book is life-enhancing, the message enticing. I am already using the skills I have learned from reading this little book."
—Joe Graves, businessman, former State Senator.

"This method works both in the classroom and in my law practice."
—Ann and George May.

"You will enjoy reading it, and learning how to improve your assertiveness in an entirely unique way, and reach a win every time, a solution with finesse.
—Maria Hubert von Staufer, author, *Jane Austen's Christmas: the Festive Season in Georgian England*, and other books.

"This useful, reader-friendly book will help anyone seeking peace and prosperity in their office, home, church, or civic organization."
—Neil Chethik, author, *FatherLoss: How sons of all ages come to terms with the deaths of their dads*

"I am certain this gentle approach allows for charitable resolutions within ministerial settings, as well within families and personal relationships."
—Rev. Cait Finnegan, priest of the Celtic Christian Church and co-director of Good Tidings.

"It's a short, simple and practical read. It's a read that can change your entire view of one tedious task—the dreaded performance review—into a mission of improving performance—yours as well as others."
—Paul Davin (retired) Vice President, Training and Development. Long John Silver's Inc. and Hardee's Food Systems Inc

Win-Win Finesse

The Art of Dealing Positively with Negative Feeling

by
Paschal Bernard Baute, Ed. D.

finesse
(fi nes') –n,
1. extreme delicacy
or subtlety in action, performance,
skill, discrimination, etc.
2. skill in handling a difficult
or highly sensitive situation;
adroit and artful management.
3. a trick, artifice, or stratagem.

*—Random House Dictionary
of the English Language,*
The Unabridged Edition, 1979

are not sure you need this book
rief two minute quiz may help.

dy for the Win-Win Finesse?

these questions with either of three answers:
U - Never; 1 = Sometimes; 2 = Often.

1. Have you had bad feelings at work or home that you did not have a good way to deal with? ____

2. Do you want to get along better with those at work but have negative feelings about the way you are treated? ____

3. Have you had a manager or boss whose behavior bothered you but you found no way to tell him? ____

4. Have you wished you were more confident or bold in speaking up with others? ____

5. Are you uncomfortable in giving honest feedback to co-workers or those you supervise? ____

6. Have you a relative whose behavior really bothers you, but you keep the family peace at all costs? ____

7. Do you hold back speaking openly for fear of hurting the feelings of those you live or work with? ____

8. Have you received criticism from someone who did not care about your feelings? ____

9. Do you desire to have a better way to deal with your negative feelings with friends? ____

10. Have you wished you were not anxious about conflict and confrontation? ____

11. Do you want more open and honest communication in your own workplace? ____

12. Are you ready to learn an effective way to deal with your negative feelings and still keep important relationships positive? ____

Add your scores. Write your score here ____
Minimum score = 0; Maximum score = 24.

Interpretation of your scores:

5 and below: **Super-cool.** You are an android; consider selling your DNA to the CIA. Return this book to the bookstore or give it to a friend "stressed-out" in work, life or love.

5-10 **Mild discomfort,** "Cool," typical levels, usually some desire to find a better way.

10-15 **Moderate discomfort,** "Warm," clear or strong desire to find a better way.

15-20 **Strong discomfort,** "Hot," ardent desire to find a better way: You are ready Now!

Those who will profit most from the reading of this book have a score of 9 or more. The higher the score, the more one is ready for learning this new, simple yet powerful way.*

* Note: This quiz has not been normed and is not valid for any other purposes than helping you ascertain whether or not you are ready for the message of the book.

Contents

Quiz

Acknowledgements..i

Foreword...iii

Introduction...v

Chapter One..................................1
End of My Rope

Chapter Two...................................5
Listening Can Be Loving

Chapter Three................................9
Some Powers Are Secret

Chapter Four................................13
When It Just Won't Work

Chapter Five................................17
Friends First

Chapter Six................................21
Practice Makes Perfect

Chapter Seven..25
My First Big Test

Chapter Eight...29
Confronting the Boss

Chapter Nine..33
May You Have an Enemy

Chapter Ten...37
Challenges for My Heart

Epilogue..43
Winning All Around

Summary of Win-Win Finesse................................47

Further Examples..49

List of the Examples......................................51

Afterword...99

About the Author...101

Guide Book for Discussion Information....................104

Order Form for the Book..................................105

Acknowledgements

The Win-Win Finesse method of constructive confrontation was perfected over the years not only with much relationship counseling but with consulting and training in conflict resolution for many companies. It was developed mutually also by two partners with strong egos who loved each other enough to trust that their negative feelings about the other's "rough edges" would be heard.

Many have given me a "hand-up" in life and work. Dedication of this work must be made to the two women who have been most significant in my life: my mother, Bertha Lilly Pratt, and my life-partner, Janette Osborne. There is no way I can express in words my indebtedness to either. Their compassion, openness and hospitality are the root of this method.

Many have offered helpful feedback in the development of this method and this book. In the discipline of Organizational Psychology, Robert A. Baker, Ph.D., Professor Emeritus, University of Kentucky, has been a consultant, mentor and friend for many years.

—Paschal Baute
October 2003

Foreword

Dr. Baute has effectively addressed the Achilles-heel in many otherwise well-run teams and organizations: the inability for people to provide negative feedback to peers, subordinates, and most important, their supervisors and managers. Based on many years of consulting with organizations, teaching conflict resolution tactics, and conducting research in this area, Dr. Baute shares his techniques and strategies for overcoming reluctance to provide negative feedback and empowers everyone to overcome their fears.

In addition to an interesting storyline, the book offers many examples from real situations to encourage readers and provides solid, time-tested tactics for improving the problem situations they find themselves in.

Readers will also find support in reading the many stories offered. They will immediately identify with the situations and realize they are not the only ones facing the situation.

This book will enhance the reader's ability to confront problems in a positive way and pave the way to a more productive, positive work environment. As such, the book will be helpful whether it is read as a "stand alone"or as a text for a college course on giving feedback or solving conflict. If everyone read this book, our workplaces would be filled with happier, more productive employees.

I highly recommend this volume for all employees, whether you are a supervisor, manager, employee, or sole-owner. Dr. Baute has made good use of his extensive experience and knowledge, and everyone stands to gain from it!

—Michael M. Harris, Ph.D.
VP, Litigation Support Services, EASI-Consult
(www.easiconsult.com),
Professor of Management, University of Missouri

Introduction

In the Old Testament, the bearer of bad news was slain. Yahweh sent Nathan the prophet to confront King David about his adultery with Bathsheba and his murder of her husband to cover up his affair. One does not easily confront kings with their sins of adultery and murder. How was Nathan to do it?

Nathan confronted the king using a story. He told a fable of the abuse of power. "In a town was a rich man and a poor man. The poor man had nothing but a ewe lamb which had become a family pet. The rich man had flocks in abundance, but when a traveler came to stay, the rich man took the poor man's lamb to prepare it for his guest." When he heard the story, King David's anger flared and he said to Nathan: "The man who did this deserves to die. He must make four fold restitution for such a thing and showing no compassion."

Nathan said to King David: "You are the man and you have shown contempt for Yahweh despite his many blessings." David repented. Nathan's use of the fable finessed the king into admitting his guilt and repenting. (II Samuel 12)

In today's competitive companies, partners at work need to give all kinds of feedback, positive and negative to one another.

Yet few people have adequate skills in confronting and dealing with their negative feelings. Still less have mastered the art and skill of constructive confrontation.

A company can have much good going for itself, good service, great products, positive attitudes, good listening, encouragement and great bottom line. Yet all this can collapse quickly when negative feelings are not dealt with constructively. Unless adequate feedback skills exist, few practice effective confronting. Conflict and poor performance do not get adequately faced. Morale and efficiency can be slowly—or rapidly—diminished.

The core competency lacking in all industries at all levels may be the ability to handle negative feelings and conflict. Without these skills, there is a diminishment of both morale and productivity—often unnoticed.

Most managers and most team members recognize that they could be more effective if they were better in handling their own negative feelings and better with feedback skills.

Feedback has been called the "breakfast of champions," by Ken Blanchard, one originator of the One Minute Manager.

The following fable is about dealing positively with negative feelings, how to set the stage so that feedback is effective, how to create a situation where it is not only accepted, but welcomed, and becomes a starting place for new open partnering.

Win-Win Finesse is about the "breakfast stuff" of champions: the milk (of caring) and cereal (bread of words), the actual breakfast food. It is about how to nourish a new workplace climate by effective feedback.

The Win-Win Finesse method employs a paradoxical communication originally developed in the double bind theory of communication theory. This method was studied at the Mental Research Institute with Paul Watzlawick in the 1980s. Since then, I have been using, teaching and perfecting this method for conflict resolution in many organizational workshops.

I believe this method is one of the most effective ways of dealing with negative feelings, conflict, and confrontation in the workplace ever discovered. This method, when well used, can help change the business world and organizational life for many persons.

Instead of living in fear and aversion of conflict and confrontation, thereby burying negative feelings, managers and associates who learn to use this method will succeed where they previously would have failed. Everyone who needs to partner in life and work can have a more effective way.

Next we take our model from the prophet Nathan and tell the reader a fable. Actually, it is only a semi-fable, as the work situations and the resolutions are actual, based on real life but disguised examples.

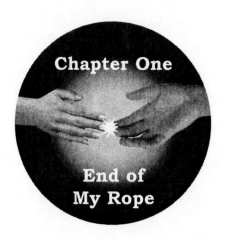

Chapter One

End of My Rope

"Road rage or maybe suicide," I muttered grimly, "is an option." Outside, wind and rain gusted against the windshield as I drove to work that October morning. Inside me, a tempest of feelings was raging. I felt ready to blow up or at the very least, make a fool of myself in some way.

Moments later, the absurdity of it all hit me and I laughed. In any crisis, I always imagine the worst case scenario. Then anything less seems a gift from God. Maybe it was being a single mom. Or maybe it was just because I was too ready to go along with others to keep the peace.

I worked in a small office with two other persons and a tough boss. We were wholesale distributors of a popular security system for home building, and usually kept two trucks busy. We were located in a shaded alcove, one story building, in Hamburg Pavilion, in Lexington, Kentucky, near Interstate 75.

I had issues with both my co-workers, Peggy and Bill. Peggy talked all the time and Bill was condescending. Meanwhile, Tom, our boss, was not easy. He was in and out of the office, completing sales. Mostly, he was a great guy, but could turn moody and critical under pressure. He had several other business projects going. Yesterday he complained that my scheduling was causing him to race from one part of the county to another. Could I please do something about that?

I simply had no idea of what to do. I hated even the hint of confrontation. I avoided disagreement with a passion, but now my stomach was churning. I had decided if I could not somehow figure a way to work it out with these three by Christmas, I would start looking for another job. Yet I also knew I would be carrying my own baggage wherever I went.

Besides the office issues, I had my ex to deal with. I knew I accommodated him too much for our daughter Emily's sake. I guess I won't even mention my mother. She is always full of advice that I seldom request. I know she means well. But why do I, Susan Young, a 32-year-old woman, still feel such a child around my mother?

On top of all this, my brother Larry, a manager, was bugging me to go back to college. He was convinced it would help me.

I was in a bind, feeling choked up, my heart in my mouth. Even away from work, I found myself rehearsing or replaying all kinds of scenarios inside my head. If I were not rehearsing one, I was replaying one.

As the team leader, I was expected to manage the work load, even though I had no official title or role. Bill was Tom's cousin and Peggy had been an old girl friend of his from high school. Bill had been Tom's right-hand man. Had been? Still was.

2

When I was hired, I was given Bill's job managing the books. When Tom announced my hiring, he said to Bill and Peggy: "Susan will keep my schedule current when I am on the road. She will also be our PR and sales backup person. She will manage the books, manage my correspondence, help you when needed, and in general keep the office working well together."

So how could I go to the boss with my dilemma, and then have both Peggy and Bill mad at me? I saw no positive outcomes possible. Mostly I was a grin and bear it kind of person. But I was on a tightrope—inwardly teetering, ready to fall into the chaos of unmanageable feelings. Fear. Frustration. Anger. Anger at my own "goes along to get along." And, feeling trapped by it all.

Headaches were beginning to hammer me with regularity. The only joy in my life was my 11 year-old daughter, Emily. After supper yesterday, she said, "Mom, you really seem down lately." She had that kind of intuition. Sheesh, my low energy level was obvious even to an eleven-year-old.

"Well, something is bothering you," she said. I shrugged my shoulders and went on preparing supper.

The past few months had taken a toll on me.

I saw proof of it again that night in the mirror. My usually sharp green eyes looked drawn and tired. I was sure there were new lines around my mouth. I knew I was not my usual perky self. I really liked my job. But what was I to do with all these unwanted feelings?

Later that night, during our goodnight hug, Emily whispered, "Mom, you need to find your own wizard. Have a dream tonight about it."

I smiled and hugged her back. I guess a Harry Potter fan is bound to believe in wizards.

I know I needed something. Wizards, fairy tales, dreams—Hah! Kids are funny. I felt my eyes fill with tears—too many feelings. Maybe I do need some kind of wizard. I had never stood up to anyone in my entire life.

As I drifted off to sleep, I hoped it would not be another restless night. October trees were now riots of color, but I was a riot of feelings.

I could not have imagined then how much my dreams were about to change my life.

Chapter Two

Listening Can Be Loving

I seemed to be on a long and perilous journey somewhere, searching intensely for what I did not know. Wearily, I climbed a mountain to a cave where resided an ancient Crone. She was sitting in a rocking chair in the shade under a crab apple tree near the cave's entrance.

I offered her a wildflower. She asked me if I understood the last dream I had. I told her that I had been scared and was running from something. She asked me if I knew what I was running from. I told her no, I did not. Then she said, "If I tell you, are you willing to risk changing, or is this just to satisfy your curiosity?"

I took a deep breath. "I am willing to risk change." I felt strange as I said those words.

She looked at me fiercely, then said "A poet wrote: 'The caged bird sings but with a fearful trill, of things unknown but longed for still[1]. . .' "

1 "Caged Bird", copyright © 1983 by Maya Angelou, from SHAKER, WHY DON'T YOU SING? by Maya Angelou. Used by permission of Random House, Inc.

At those words, my insides abruptly ached. Was it I? My breathing seemed to stop. Finally I managed to get out the words, "What in the world do you mean?"

"You are running from what you fear. You are afraid of negative feelings—both your own and others."

How could she read my heart so clearly?

Part of this, I admit, I already knew. Growing up chubby–always feeling like an outsider, I felt as if I had never fully arrived as an adult.

Suddenly, my defenses crumbled. I felt wave after wave of feeling hit me: anxiety, fear, grief, anger and yet, in the midst of it all, a small hint of, could it be, hope?

"Am I afraid of something in particular?" I finally dared to ask.

After a pause and a glance that seemed to lance me, she spoke, "You are afraid that if you stand up to your ex, he will withdraw his love from Emily. So you often bite your lip and swallow your feelings."

I sighed. In my heart I felt myself saying, "Yes."

"You are afraid that if you are more open about your negative feelings, people will not like you."

Ouch! That hurt. But she was right. Too right. "The caged bird sings with a fearful trill, of things unknown but longed for still." Her words pierced me, but maybe, a huge festering wound had been lanced. Was I the wound? I felt eerie but wondrous: things unknown but longed for still. Like being on the verge of something I could not name.

I took a deep breath, and the largest breath I ever took. "Please help me," I said.

She looked at me fiercely with eyes that seemed to go to my innermost depths. "I will teach you a way to learn to confront others while at the same time valuing your relationship with them," she said. "And I will show you how to tell your feelings in a way that makes it hard for the other person to get upset at whatever you say."

I could hardly believe what she was saying. But there was something else she called for.

She continued, "First, I must have your agreement. You must agree to teach it to someone else. The best way we learn anything is to explain it to others, then DO it."

"Yes, okay."

She had a warning, "This is a very valuable tool and it can be easily misused, as humans are likely to do with anything. So you must teach it rightly and only to those who will use it properly."

I agreed. "And I assume you will show me how to do this."

After a long pause–she seemed to be deciding whether to continue—she said, "You learn to do this because you value your relationships. You appreciate them. This is the very first point. This is a caring confrontation. It must always be done at eye level, accepting the other as an equal, and respecting that everyone is different from us. I will explain it to you. Then, give you examples of how this Way is not to be used."

"Go ahead," I said somewhat impatiently.

"Do you understand first that listening—listening well—is an act of love?"

"Act of love?" My first reaction was 'Absurd!'

"Even at work?" I asked. "My co-worker talks endlessly."

"Even at work. When you allow the differing point

of view of the other to be present to your awareness, this is an act of love. You have to make way for their view to be truly heard, which means putting aside, even if only for a moment, your own agenda, your own internal busyness."

"But this is hard work!" I protested, remembering differences with my ex.

"Yes. Not all people are ready for it."

"Okay," I said. "I can see that. But why all this explanation?"

"Because what I am about to teach you is really powerful. It can be widely misused. Especially by people who pride themselves on being 'tough-minded.' And who are direct, decisive, impatient, and always after results."

I waited.

"Because not everyone is ready to use this Way and some may never be. A few are likely to say something like, 'I need to talk to you, and you are not going to like it.' This is a patronizing put-down."

"What do you call this method?" I asked, curious.

"We call it The Way."

"Tell me what it is and how to do it!" I pleaded.

But the figure disappeared in an instant. I woke up. The dream was over.

All day long I mused about my dream. Was I really the caged bird? If true, then only I could open the door to the cage. I thought about her words and how not to do it. I wondered what would be the right way. "Caged bird singing with a fearful trill...." The words began to haunt me.

My Crone spirit had snared my interest.

Chapter Three

Some Powers Are Secret

The next day was like I was in a walking trance. I got through it. That night I met the Crone again in my dream. She was hoeing her garden. She seemed more ancient, wise and more beautiful than the first time. She looked up as I approached and smiled. I remembered I had not asked her name.

"Mechtilda is my name," she said, "But there is a secret power in my name and you must not give away my secret until you have mastered The Way thoroughly."

"Are you ready to explain the secret to me?" I asked.

"Just about," she said. "How many times have you been confronted by anyone who started out being sensitive to your feelings?"

I thought about it—but not for long. "Actually, Never," I replied.

"The first secret power of The Way is simply this notably overlooked approach. You begin by explaining that because you value the relationship, because you appreciate them, you need to talk about something. But

you are concerned that this may hurt their feelings. Then you pause, willing to wait for a go-ahead. Tell me when you start this way, what have you done?"

"Well, I began by explaining that I am doing this because I care about the person's feelings?"

"Precisely, but much more."

"Got 'em really curious and wondering," I replied.

"Much more," she insisted.

"On guard, at least a little . . . "

"Yes, but more!"

"I dunno . . . " I said.

"Now listen carefully. When someone predicts you will probably do something, what is your likely natural response?"

"To say to myself, 'Ha! I will show you that you are wrong!' Then I will lean over backwards to prevent the prediction about me from coming true." I paused. "I will be determined to prove them wrong," I said.

"Exactly. That is the second hidden power in this. By caring about their feelings and predicting a possible negative response, you have finessed the negative response making it unlikely that it will happen. Not impossible, mind you—but unlikely."

"Finesse? What do you mean by finesse?" I asked.

"Finesse is simply a subtle and shrewd way to get someone to do something they might ordinarily not do—like a little honey with the medicine, so to speak. Here it is like a little honey mustard flavoring, tasty enough that they can't resist the challenge."

"Hmmm," I murmured. Could what she was saying really work?

"This is what we call the 'positive double-bind,'" she continued. "Negative double bind is a Catch-22. But this is a positive double-bind because your prediction itself has made it unlikely that the negative response will occur."

"Wow," I said. "It really seems simple. Does it always work?"

She laughed. "Nothing works 100 percent of the time with humans. But done properly it will work about 80 percent of the time. It will often work even when you have used it before and the person knows what you are doing—if you have an ongoing good relationship with them. There are a few cases when it will not work. I will explain these later."

"So I start out by saying that my listener will have difficulty handling what I want to say?"

"Yes, but there is another secret needed to make this work."

I just looked at her expectantly.

She said, "Next you say, 'And maybe now is not a good time?' Then pause. Allow them to say whether the present moment is the best time. By this pause, you are requesting specific permission to continue. Sometimes a person may say, 'I am too busy right now.' But you certainly have their attention, and they will usually get back to you soon. Usually most will say, 'Go ahead.'"

"I can't believe it is this easy," I said.

"Neither can many others, until they have tried it," she said, smiling. "But there is one smaller secret that can 'seal the deal' still better with some people. After asking whether this is the best time for them, you add an aside and say, 'And this is not easy for me either.'"

"What does that do?" I asked.

"It serves to put you really at eye level. It's a cue for you to know whether you are doing this mechanically in a patronizing way. If it is not true, then you are not truly eye level. That is, you are using The Way in an automatic fashion, believing there is some power in the words—rather than in the power of caring. If it is really not easy for you, this means that you are sincere. And you are willing to accept whatever is the outcome of your attempt, and will still listen."

At this point I realized that I was not listening well. My mind was already jumping ahead to scenarios at my office, imagining how it surely would not work with Peggy, Bill or Tom.

"What are the cases in which this will not work?" I asked, being sure that my partners and boss at work would be the impossible types. There had to be a downside. I looked for the worst in any situation.

Mechtilda only smiled.

Then I awoke. It seemed so unreal yet like it had a life of its own. Would I open the door to my cage? Was I ready? I had no idea where this was taking me.

Chapter Four

When It Just Won't Work

After work the next day, I told my daughter Emily that I was dreaming about a wizard. Naturally she wanted to know all about it. But I wasn't ready to share any of it yet with anyone. The Crone's words were haunting my every waking hour. Yet the dreams seemed to be helping. I was afraid that if I talked about it, I might break the magic that seemed to have found me.

The third night I slept without dreaming and was disappointed. Then I decided that maybe my dreamlessness was merely the extra slice of pizza I had or wanting too much to visit my wise old Crone.

But on the fourth night, I found her again.

Mechtilda was again outside her cave, tending a variety of pretty flowers. All her own colors seemed to be autumn–eyes, skin, hair–even her robe was a deep and rich brown. She turned to look at me as I approached.

She offered me a flower, smiling. I took it and said, "Are you ready to tell me when the Way will not work?"

"Yes," she said, and this time she did not hesitate.

"First, it will not work with a person with whom you have a fearful or suspicious relationship. There must be some caring and some trust to even engage. You may have to build some appreciation first with this person. You must find some common bond with them."

I thought of my ex. Maybe this applied to him–or to both of us?

"Secondly, it does not usually work with teenagers, although I have a couple of moms and dads who are proving me wrong. Nothing much works well with them because they must each find their own path."

Gee, I thought to myself I do not want to hear that about teenagers. I have a daughter too close. I was already sweating this biological necessity, doing my thing, sometimes imagining worst case scenarios about her.

Mechtilda went on.

"Thirdly, it does not work with those who pride themselves on being tough minded, no-nonsense types, who are decisive and independent. When you start with them, they are likely to interrupt and say, 'Please get to the point, cut to the chase.' They are suspicious about feelings. Feelings for them are fuzzy-wuzzies–a soft side of themselves they prefer not to attend."

"They are also the type of person who will not use The Way well—whom I described earlier to you. If they try, they will use the words as a formula, and think they have done all that is necessary to set the stage for it to work."

She paused, then continued.

"They have missed the heart of it because they do not use the heart."

"Are they hopeless?" I asked.

"Dreamland research is continuing," she said. *"Some may be. Some may not be. People can change. "*

"Is that all?" I asked.

"No," she said, *"There seem to be a few others that this Way will simply not work with at all. They seem to be the ones who cannot handle ANY confrontation. It is too much of an insult to their identity for them to accept that others do not think or feel as they do. "*

"Are they many?" I asked.

"Only a few. Maybe one out of 20 or 30 persons."

"Why are they like that?" I was curious.

She was quiet for a moment, then said "They believe since they are sincere, they cannot be wrong."

She smiled. "They wear sincerity like a suit of armor. Sincerity is their inoculation against any view that would challenge their view of themselves."

Once more, I confess that I thought of my ex. Couldn't help it. Sorry. Why do I sometimes find myself apologizing to myself?

"Are these kind of people hard to live with?" I could not get past this point.

"Sadly, some are so closed that they require others around them to live a secret life. Others must learn to keep things inside to get along. It is the opposite of The Way."

"Oh boy," I thought, *"How true." Then I thought, that was the way my ex and I had ended. Maybe both of us felt that way about the other. Sad. Suddenly I was lost in remembering hurts. There was a long pause.*

Finally I said, "So, now, wise one, am I ready?"

"Only after you have explained it and taught it to one other person first."

"How will this help?"

"You learn anything well by teaching it to others."

"Okay," I said.

"One more secret," she added. "The place is important. Whenever possible, do this over lunch. Food sets a different tone, a more positive climate."

"That makes sense," I said. "What is the other?"

"When I see you are making The Way work, I will visit you in another dream to share another secret with you. It is part of the graduate course," and she smiled.

"Thank you," I said.

"You are welcome."

And then—she was gone again.

I woke. The next day I started writing down all that I remembered. It seemed too unreal. Could dreams really be that helpful? Was I in some kind of waking trance? If so, I was not ready for it to end. Maybe what I was learning were the tools I needed to unlock my cage. No–to become uncaged. Imagining that was a funny-strange feeling.

Chapter Five

Friends First

I wrote a lot the first few days—partially to avoid doing anything different, partially because I was afraid I would forget what was in the dream. I wanted to remember as much as possible.

I did explain it to one good friend. She was very interested and said she would be curious how it worked out. Explaining it to her, helped make clear the positive double bind part of the Finesse.

I had written:

1. When someone predicts that we are likely to do something, the natural tendency is to lean over backwards to prove them wrong. It's a reactive response. The internal response is "Who says I can't? I will show you!"

2. In this situation, the quickest way we can gain control of someone predicting something about us is to prove them wrong by not behaving in the way they just predicted we would.

3. Therefore, when someone predicts a negative response from us in a caring way, we are challenged to avoid the negative response and to give the speaker a positive reception. This makes it a win-win outcome for both parties.

The core values seem to be:
• Wanting to work through barriers to get to better team work
• Caring about feelings because we appreciate the friendship
• Respecting the readiness of the other person
• Pacing any feedback given with tact and diplomacy

Then I got tired of writing. I was both impatient to try the new method, yet still too anxious to try it at work. Maybe "scared" was a more honest word. I knew I had to change something. I worried for almost a week, "Whom I should start this with?"

I finally decided to risk it first with my sister-in-law, Jackie. First, we are such good friends that if I flopped I might be forgiven. Secondly, I let her really "get to me" and don't say anything. Which bothers me, and I let it spoil an evening together. And sometimes I take it to bed with me.

Then I fretted on-and-off three more days how I could begin this with her.

Even though her brother and I divorced two years ago, Jackie has remained a good friend. She and I were so close that I never considered her my "former" sister-in-law. Jackie and I share a lot because we are both single moms with similar problems. Maybe because we have shared so much is one reason I like her.

But Jackie is "bossy" and offers me advice even when I don't ask for it. She even knows she is "bossy," but it doesn't seem to bother her. Where it bothers me is when she gets very critical of my ex.

Jackie and I often spent an evening per week together, discussing life, love, movies, housework, kids, parents and siblings. In the past I have not spoken up when she criticized Ed even though I usually got very tense. Whenever she did this, it set a different tone for the evening.

So my first attempt was with Jackie. If I failed with her, it would not make any difference. I needed to stop being anxious when she gave me that free advice. Actually, I needed to stop her from giving me that free advice. I decided to tell her my honest feelings about the way she felt so free to criticize her brother and my response to him.

I took a deep breath. "Jackie, I appreciate our friendship. I want to talk with you about something, but I am concerned that you may not like it and may even resent my speaking up."

"Have I done something wrong?" she asked.

"No, not really," I said. "We talk about many things that I enjoy. But I get upset when you start criticizing Ed. I have to get along with him for Emily's sake. I would prefer Ed not to come up in our conversation again. You and I talk about anything and everything with each other–which I like. (I paused.) I really prefer that talk about Ed be off-limits."

I had practiced saying this but now found it hard to believe I was actually saying the words. Then I held my breath. I had never been that direct with anyone in my entire life. What would she think and feel toward me? Because she is usually very free in expressing herself, I expected she might get upset with me.

Much to my surprise, she just sat there for a few moments (it seemed forever to me) and then she said, "Okay, Susan. I will respect your feelings. I will do my best not to talk about Ed. Besides, we have so many other things we talk about–that's no big loss!" Then she laughed, "Are you ready for the pizza yet?" Jackie usually made up her mind quickly about things, and said so.

Suddenly, my worst case scenario with Jackie seemed silly.

I could hardly believe it worked so easily. Later, I thought that just having the Win-Win plan gave me the courage to speak up on an issue that had been bothering me. Maybe I did not need to rehearse worst case scenarios before risking new behavior.

I had opened the door to my caged bird. Maybe I was perched on the doorstep looking around, almost ready to fly. Was I ready to try this at work?

Chapter Six

Practice Makes Perfect

October leaves were beginning to fall after the heavy rain. It was a new week and a sunny Monday when I decided to begin with Peggy, the talker. This time I worried less about it before doing it—only for two days. Of my three work challenges, she seemed the easiest. I enjoyed the fact that she and I talked a lot in the office and were good friends. But I felt like Peggy dumped on me a lot with her negative feelings. I have probably been too good a listener while not wanting to rock the boat. I had become the sounding board for all her complaints.

I invited her to lunch. After we broke bread, I said: "Peggy, I really enjoy talking with you and the way we work together, but there is something I need to discuss. I am hesitant to do so because I don't want to hurt your feelings." I paused and looked at her. She looked curious and concerned. Then I said, "This may not be the best time." She said, "What could be a better time than this?"

I told her that I valued her friendship. Then I paused, realizing this was only the second time in my life I had risked doing this. She waited. I finally blurted it out, "Peggy, while usually I enjoy talking with you, I do not enjoy hearing all the negative things about your husband, children, pets, in-laws, weather, friends or anything."

At first, she seemed shocked by my words. I added, "Maybe it was partially my fault in the past by being such a good listener, but maybe we just got into a bad habit." I said I thought that at work we could start the day off better.

When the initial shock faded, Peggy became very apologetic. She kept insisting that she did not realize she was doing this so often. She said I should have brought this to her attention sooner and I agreed this was so. She promised to work very hard to keep this kind of talk to a minimum.

Over the week since our lunch together, our conversations seem a little strained—like she was a little guarded in what she said. But I know the foundation is there for more honest and successful communication in the future.

My worst case scenario with Peggy simply vaporized.

With this second win, I began to feel some genuine confidence in myself. Maybe I was not condemned always to hide my negative feelings. Maybe I wasn't a hopeless dove like one sassy girlfriend once called me. Maybe I did not need to fret endlessly before speaking up. The caged bird was out. Maybe this Way could really work.

I told my brother Larry about what I was trying to do (but not about the Crone). He seemed pleased and replied, "Susan, you are taking responsibility for yourself and for your environment. That is the beginning of leadership." That made me proud. My brother was not usually one for compliments.

Win Win Finesse

Chapter Seven

My First Big Test

After the Win-Win Finesse worked with Peggy, my confidence in my ability to use it bloomed. Meanwhile, I had been worrying about Tom's complaint. When at last I hit on the solution, it was so obvious and plain that I laughed.

Bill handled telephone sales. He was often late and left early. In my opinion, he was not keeping up with the territory. When I had to handle his calls, I'd get complaints about him not calling back. It was his job as well as mine to set up outside sale visits for the boss. As executive secretary, I was supposedly also team leader, but I never had any orientation and it was not in my job description. Moreover, I had avoided all conflict.

My solution was that if Bill were more on top of his job, and gave me more lead time for the boss to make outside sales, then I could schedule the boss by county areas. In other words, south on Tuesday, west on Wednesday and so on. Then Tom wouldn't be racing from one side of the county to the other all the time. Since Bill was family to him and preceded me on the job, I told Tom my plan first and asked if I could talk with Bill about it. "Go for it," he said encouragingly.

Now, my other issue with Bill was that he had always seemed condescending with me. He did not seem keen on my running the office. The other stuff: doing the books, handling the web page, being backup, PR and newsletters was okay. But in charge of the office? I could tell he resented it.

I needed a good plan. The problem was that Bill was accustomed to giving the sales calls directly to Tom. Then I collected the ones also from Peggy and phone-ins from previous customers and passed them on. No one person was keeping a central schedule for Tom to follow.

I decided to lay the problem in Bill's lap. This time I fretted less before beginning with Bill as I had a solution to an office problem. I told him about Tom's complaint to me. I was almost sure Bill would not volunteer to be the sole scheduler for Tom. I said I had an idea but needed his input and would need his complete cooperation to make it work. He looked at me and said, "What is it?"

"Bill, we need to have a better scheduling system for Tom. Currently he's running from one end of the county to the other because we are not sorting the calls into one area or region at a time."

"That seems a good analysis," said Bill. "Go on."

"I need to say something here that may upset you, (I paused) and now may not be the best time?" Bill just said, "Go ahead."

"I know that you get behind in your calls sometimes, because I fill in for you some mornings and late afternoons, and some customers have complained that you have not gotten back to them."

I paused for that to sink in, half-holding my breath and hoping he would not notice. Who was I to tell Bill how to do his job? He was a poker-face guy and he showed no emotion.

"I understand that you need to call Tom directly at times, with new sales calls, but this also lets me out of the loop." I paused. "If we were to schedule Tom's calls by the area—north, south, east and west on a particular day of the week, he could make six or seven calls per day rather than three to five. It would also be easier to track Tom if one person alone is the scheduler."

I paused again. "What do you think? You would have a higher sales commission, and Tom would be covering each area of the county, day by day, in turn?" I knew this would require Bill to stay on top of his calls and anticipate better.

I almost held my breath. I mused that there is more than one way to skin a rabbit, as my uncle used to say. To my surprise, Bill said, "I think that is a good idea, Susan. I appreciate your coming up with this solution. I think I can help in the scheduling plan. Why did you think that would upset me?" he asked.

It is okay with me if Bill wanted to pretend that the new arrangement would not require him to be more timely.

"I guess I was wrong in expecting that you might think I was elbowing in on your relationship with Tom," I said, and smiled my best smile. I shrugged my shoulders. "I am glad you like it."

Another of my worst case scenarios collapsed!

"In fact," said Bill, "I think it is worth trying. And will make things go more smoothly here in the office as well. I will not have to play catch up with Tom hour by hour when a new call comes in. I can pass it on to you and concentrate on my own calls."

"Good," I said, barely breathing, still hoping that I had gotten through this dialogue with Bill without any fireworks. For some reason, I thought he might get upset and think I was trying to tell him how to do his job.

To say the least, I was very pleased with myself. Could this really be working? Had my worst case scenarios protected me from failure or possibly blocked me from taking risks?

As I thought about it later, I felt almost ready to take on my boss. The caged bird was out hopping around, taking short mini-flights from one part of the room to another, exploring new territory. But not yet sure she had the wings to fly anywhere.

Chapter Eight

Confronting the Boss

A week later, the new scheduling was working well. I had scored one with the boss.

I was not doing anything else different at the office, but I realized I was feeling less stressed and more confident. Once I figured that I did not need to avoid all conflict and disagreement, it is amazing how much a burden seemed to lift from my heart.

Furthermore, I found I was OK with not liking some things about some people which before I could not let myself admit. It is funny what a difference practicing one little skill was making in my overall attitude.

Did I say "little?" Mechtilda would laugh. Maybe I will also laugh at such a "simple" complexity once I have mastered it.

I was wondering how much worrying I needed to do before taking on my boss. Instead of weeks, maybe only a day or so. I decided I was almost ready. Then I stalled another couple of days. Finally I said to myself: what the heck–just do it! So far, things had worked better than I dreamed they would. But, as I thought more about it, I decided 'twas better to catch him on one of his up days. I chose Wednesday. The middle of the week I figured was safer.

This was the big one, I told myself. A few weeks earlier I could not have imagined myself doing this. Ever.

Leaves were falling everywhere when I walked into his office early one Wednesday in November. "Tom," I said, "can we talk?"

He did not look up. Instead he said, "I have three projects for you to get done this morning. All urgent. We can talk this afternoon."

Uh-uh. Was this an omen?

"Okay," I said. This afternoon would be fine.

Now how will I keep myself from rehearsing worst case scenarios with Tom till then? I took a long restroom break.

Then I decided I could run some other tapes inside my head. One of the few things Ed and I enjoyed was skiing together. I had only taken it up to please him. No risk taker, I skied a lot more conservatively, but I never fell even though somehow I managed to keep up with him. I decided to run some ski memories, movies inside my head, during the morning. Beautiful scenes. Outdoors in the wintertime. The fun we had. No pain—no gain. No guts—no glory. No balls—no blue chips. I knew it was now or never with my boss. I could hardly believe I was ready to do this. But I had decided that I was now as ready as I would ever be.

I completed the required projects cheerfully running my internal ski movies. Later that afternoon I came to his office, and asked, "Is now a good time?" Inside I was not cool.

He motioned me to a chair. I sat down. He

stayed behind his desk. I did not want Tom behind his desk where he could answer the phone and we could be interrupted. I also did not want to talk to him in his position as boss. It is hard enough to talk with someone over you in authority.

I said, "This is personal," and with my eyes and head nodded to the chair beside me. He got up and came around the desk and sat down. His eyes were on me.

"Tom, I know you work hard, and there are work pressures that I cannot even dream about. But there is something I need to talk about which is hard for me." (pause)

"You are a good boss and I do not want to hurt your feelings."

"Please go ahead, Susan," he said.

Then and there in the middle of it, I got afraid of what I was about to do. Were we most scared just before new steps? When I remembered my previous successes, my fear began to melt. I felt encouraged. Now I could proceed. With my heart almost in my mouth, I jumped in.

"There are times, Tom, when you are really moody, like a bear, grouchy, irritable, picky like nothing can please you. Then we try hard to stay out of your way." It was out. I had actually said it to my boss. My breathing almost stopped in the instant after that, waiting.

"Really?" said Tom, reflectively. "I did not think it was that often."

"About once a week," I said, beginning to breathe again. "Usually a Thursday or Friday, sometimes a Monday. Maybe your schedule is starting to eat you," I said smiling, relieved. Could this actually be working?

Tom looked very thoughtful. After a few moments, he smiled back. "Susan, I am glad you brought this to my attention. I can do better. I do not want my business worries to affect the work climate here in the office. I think you are doing a great job, by the way."

This sounded like an opening so I took it. "Well, remember when you introduced me to our office staff, you said I want Susan to help manage this and coordinate things in this office."

"Well, none of that is in my job description. So sometimes I do not know if I am over stepping my limits, 'my authority,' so to speak."

"Well," Tom said, "if you have a problem, you can just come in and talk like you did today."

Well, this was not really what I wanted. But hey, Susan. One small step at a time. I decided I was not ready to push it.

We talked about a couple of other things before I left. As I got up to leave, I felt like today was a real win for this conflict-avoider. I had things out on the table with Tom. No big solutions, but at least he knew my feelings and had offered an open door for a new part of me.

I smiled all the way home. I looked in the mirror that evening and admired my reflection. I saw a relaxed and happy face. I even seemed younger, my eyes more alive. I was beginning to feel different at work too–more relaxed and more a part of a team. The sense of partnership I now had with everyone was growing.

No longer caged, my heart was singing a new song.

Chapter Nine

May You Have an Enemy

Things were going so much better at work, I could hardly believe it. November chill was upon us, but it seemed warmer in the office.

Tom's sales were up 12 percent in the first three weeks. He kept contact with me during the day with his cell phone so we could add calls that were in the county area where he already was. Bill was more regular with his hours. He was less coming in late and leaving earlier. He also seemed to be less condescending toward me.

I made a note that, with my new skill and confidence, I might need to face that issue in time, which before would have been an impossible obstacle for me.

My relationships with Peggy and Jackie were better than ever. We laughed more easily at our own mishaps and foibles. We seemed more free with each other.

I began to wonder what the "graduate course" was that Mechtilda had promised, the other secret.

Was my Crone spirit finessing my worst case scenario tapes?

It seemed a long time before I had another dream about her. But, suddenly in a dream, there she was.

She was sitting once more in her rocking chair. I greeted her and thanked her. I told her my life was much better. She smiled and nodded. She seemed to know intuitively what was in my heart.

She seemed to be so fully present to me in the dream, like her heart to my heart. It was as if she had an almost unguarded heart. I was not sure at times whether the conversations were spoken or merely felt.

"Are the words you have given me so important that I must always use these particular words?" I asked.

"Oh my goodness, no," she said, and laughed. "Some people have been doing things like this for years. Some simply prefer to say, 'Suzie, I care about our relationship, but you are ticking me off. Do you want to know why?'"

She looked at me as though to see whether I caught the joke. After a moment, she laughed. I laughed. We laughed together at the unbending gruffness.

Then I remembered a big hurt—what my ex-husband, also a quiet man and conflict-avoider, finally said to me after nine years of marriage. I said aloud, "Or, Susan, you bug the s–t out of me, do you want to know why?"

We both laughed again, though I started to get misty and sad.

"That's a bit more colloquial," she said. "But we both know why this is not a true finesse and why it will not work, don't we?"

"Yes," I said simply, and thought "No heart, no finesse"

She took a deep breath and looked fully into my eyes.

"I think you are ready for the final secret," she said.

"You mean there is only one more?" I asked.

"Oh, no. Life is full of secrets. You can't learn them all at once. One 'final' one for now," she said.

I waited.

"Every good person deserves an enemy," she said.

I could not really grasp the meaning. I repeated it to myself to get it to sink in. Then I repeated the words slowly out loud. "Every good person? Deserves? An enemy?"

"Everyone deserves someone who will stretch them," she finally said. "Otherwise we do not grow. We remain in our comfort zone."

I still looked puzzled.

"Only if someone is against us in some way are we forced to get out of our box, forced to look for a new way to look at the world, our world," she said.

I was trying to grasp all this. It was not easy.

"'Reframing' is what it is called. Examples are: 'It could be worse.' 'What doesn't kill you—can make you stronger.' 'It is not a problem but a challenge.' 'Life is the Great Teacher.'"

With that, suddenly, I knew exactly what she meant. The relevance of all that had been happening to me became clear.

I felt joy, and relief. Enormous relief. Another load lifted.

"Of course," I said. This was precisely what I have been learning. I could reframe conflict as an opportunity for growth. And now I had some skills.

"Yes, you have avoided conflict because you feared the worst. Have you learned that the mind does not judge the heart well, that things seldom turn out as bad as you expected?" she asked.

Again my Crone was right on.

"Both good and bad," she said. "We overestimate how we will feel. It is never as bad nor quite as good as we expected, right?"

I thought to myself, "Girl, that could sure explain a lot in my life!" I had spent a lot of energy protecting myself. In fact, I had not been a good forecaster of my feelings.

Then she was gone. .

"Wait," I called out. I did not want her to go so fast.

But she was gone. The dream was over.

I was sad, but not for long. The next evening I told Emily that I was beginning to believe in Wizards.

"Betcha mine are smarter than yours!" she said, and laughed.

Knowing the vividness of her imagination but the new power of my own dreams, I just said "Maybe," and laughed, too. It was a belly laugh. I realized that I was laughing more freely, actually more often. I was finding more humor in things that happened. I searched and found my most colorful sweater to wear. The freed bird was beginning to sing with abandon.

Chapter Ten

Challenges for My Heart

Tree limbs were bare everywhere, November was almost over, sweater and coat-time, when Mechtilda appeared to me again in another dream.

She told me there were more secrets. I asked what they were. She said they would be revealed to me in time, only when I had been faithful to all she had taught me.

Then the Crone said to me, "Susan—"

This felt strange because I did not remember her ever calling my name before. Was I more of a person now?

"Susan, I do have a tip. You will find your own rhythm and grace only when you have used this method with five different people. Five."

"Five?" I asked, surprised at the number.

"Well, really seven is needed to attain grace in action. But you live in an American fast-food, hurry-up-everything society. So for you, we say 'five.'" She was smiling as if this were some kind of private knowledge in her world. "You are an impatient lot, " she added, looking directly at me.

Then she turned as if to leave. I stepped forward

and grabbed her sleeve. I wanted to wrestle her for one more revelation.

"Wait a minute, Mechtilda!" I realized it was the first time I had called her by name. "Why do you call this The Way?"

She looked at me with her eyes afire, seeming delighted with my question. "Because it includes many values of the wisdom traditions of the world." She paused. "These you can figure out for yourself. I will suggest only two. Because it can bring a new gentleness into anywhere people work, live or love. Because we all have a blind side to ourselves and this way gives people a loving way to deal with that."

With that she seemed to be leaving. I did not want her to go. I reached for her sleeve again to hold her, but she drew back. Then suddenly she came close, and reaching with her left hand, touched my heart. One final word, I begged inwardly, still not wanting her to leave.

Then she said, "Okay, Susan, I have three hard questions that your heart might not be ready for."

Then she was gone. Really gone.

"That's not fair!" I said out loud. It should be up to me to decide whether I am ready to answer questions. "My heart is not ready for?" Things my mind was ready for that my heart was not? What could that be? The dream ended with my being most curious.

Later, when awake, I decided Mechtilda was asking me to decide first whether my heart was ready to risk before she actually asked anything of me. How did my Crone know that I had never been much of a risk-taker? Did she dare to ask me to decide to risk before telling me what the risk was? Is that some kind of trick? For this cautious one, that should be an easy one to put on the back burner and simply forget about.

Later still I found myself thinking, "Well, Susan, four down—when will be the next?" To my surprise, I found it pleasant to anticipate who the next person might be, with a sense of confident readiness. A day later when driving to work, I realized something else. "I am really ready now to be more up-front with my ex." I even found myself feeling gentler toward him. After all, if he had kept things inside until he exploded at me, what had I been about to do with others?

Surprise, surprise.

What a difference a dream can make! My world today felt like an afternoon in Spring just after the rain had refreshed every living thing.

Emily came home from school yesterday and announced, "I have a boy friend."

"Oh?" I said, feeling "oops," and hiding my scare.

"Yep! We discovered we both loved the latest adventure of Harry Potter."

Well, things could be worse, I mused and smiled.

When I smiled now, I had a secret. My own secret. I knew my Crone spirit was at home in my heart—also smiling. I did not realize then how fully, yet how wonderfully, my life would be still challenged, nor how I would come to love the challenges.

Then I tried this method on my brother Larry.

Number five! It worked! He was twice amused, once because it worked on him, and then because it was I, his sister, being unusually assertive. He smiled and said, "Susan, you now have fire in your gentleness." I like that. Can I own that–fire in my gentleness? Could my brother count as my fifth try?

Finally–it seemed ages—I dreamed of Mechtilda once more.

"Are you ready for the three questions?" she said. I had almost forgotten.

Yes, it had been on the back burner, but over the past few weeks, I had decided that I was ready to risk. I was enormously curious. "Yes, please," part of me about to quiver.

"Are you ready now to trust your chaos, without running worst case scenarios?"

Curious question, I thought. "Why should I?" I demanded.

"Because now you realize it is new life emerging. You no longer need worst case scenarios."

"You mean I no longer need to protect myself by worst case scenarios?" Well, that was a heart question, I mused. Actually I had been thinking about this. I realized that chaos was chaos only when one viewed it as chaos. My upset feelings were not the automatic triggers for my worst case scenarios. I could choose to sort out the feelings. But I was not sure I was ready to give up this familiar habit completely. It was like an old friend.

"I dunno. I am not sure." I hedged, "what is the second question?"

She paused. "Are you now ready to forgive Ed?"

Oops! Well, I was certainly feeling different about

him already. I knew I needed to stop running bad mem-ory tapes. I also had figured that if I forgave him, it would not be for his sake, but for my own sake. It made no sense to keep waiting for him to change. This really was a heart question—maybe a question for a big heart? I was realizing that I had more than one cage I had kept myself in.

"What is the third question?" I dared to ask.

She paused and looked at me again with that penetrating look of hers that seemed utterly to pierce me.

"Are you ready now to be open to the possibility of love in your life?"

I knew what she meant. Oh! I reached for my heart. I was certainly feeling very different about myself these days.

Larry had told me that if I were to love Emily rightly I needed to have some male companionship. I had dismissed his advice as "typical machismo." Were they both right?

I thought about it. Oh! These were all heart ques-tions–heart challenges, for sure.

Then, out of nowhere, I actually felt a huge acceptance welling up from deep down—coming from a reservoir of all the good feelings from all that I had been doing. A burst of sunlight after an early winter's first dusting of snow—with birds announcing their joy. Was this some vision being disclosed to me? Did all change need to come from some place deep inside first? Maybe my own change had started when I felt I had to risk finding a way to escape the misery of the cage I was in. Mechtilda was asking me to risk still more—of my heart.

I took a deep breath, looked at her and said:
"Here are my answers, Mechtilda, to your three heart questions: 'Yes, yes, and. . . .YES!'"

Then I woke. When I woke, I blinked tears of gladness in my eyes–a full heart. Oh, yes! My heart was freed! My day now seemed a song. No, I was the song—a new song.

I felt like dancing, like it was somebody's birth day! Imagine me! When I looked outside that morning, I saw lovely snowflakes.

Epilogue

Winning
All Around

Recently, as the holidays grew near, I joined a "Communications at Work" class in a local business school for non-traditional students. These are people like me who have full time jobs. I thought what Larry was encouraging me to do would simply be a lot of hard work. I did not realize that going back to school could be so much fun and that I would meet so many interesting people.

Also, I was much less stressed at work—no longer anxious about misunderstandings, disagreement, or conflict. I did not feel the need to talk things out with someone while tied always with my fear of confrontation.

Meanwhile, since I loved browsing the Internet, I was also studying "double bind" and "conflict resolution" on the web and taking notes. I decided to tell my new class about this finesse way. Maybe I could use my experience as one of my required reports.

So I summarized what I was learning for the class:
• In a negative double bind, one is damned if one does and damned if one doesn't. The novel

Catch 22 is a perfect example. In a positive double bind, you are challenged to respond positively to a negative prediction to prove the one predicting your negative response wrong. This creates a win-win interaction by finessing any possible negative response.
• The receiver 'wins' by accepting the feedback graciously and proving the predictor wrong, and thereby claims more control of the situation. The one giving the feedback has skillfully arranged for his 'prediction' to turn out wrong, by offering a 'one-up' to the receiver. Further, the receiver is the one who chooses the time and place for it to be received–also giving him or her control. The stage is set for the receiver choosing to "buy in" —in a dramatic enough way that the challenge is unforgettable, even if it should be delayed.
• The one making the confrontation has delivered the message of feedback in a caring and diplomatic way that insures good working together in the future. The goal is to maintain good relationships. At that point both are now ready to work together more cooperatively.

As we discussed these points in class, what became clear to everyone was that not only is that particular relationship stronger, but the teamwork becomes stronger. The company is also stronger, because a new model or paradigm for working together effectively has been demonstrated. It becomes a win for all parties. It increases the give and take and effective partnering under almost all conditions.

Well, the class sure liked it and had many questions. Then, after more discussion, I realized something else, but only about a week later. Another surprise happened, a "Wow!" This came after I realized that I was actually feeling "gentle" toward Bill, something I could not have imagined earlier. The surprise was that it was changing ME as well as the others.

The method brought both parties into a positive double bind, not just the one being given the feedback. So it was actually a double-double bind, winning all around.

In other words, I discovered that my use of the Win-Win Finesse was having an effect on my attitude. I was being finessed out of my negative feelings, really out of imagining worst case scenarios, by the finesse method.

This is what I think happens: once I declare that I appreciate the relationship enough to risk bringing up negative feelings while being concerned about the other's feelings, then hesitate to proceed without explicit permission, I have made it harder for me to get upset at the other's response. I have given control of the outcome to the other while remaining responsive.

This magnifies the likelihood of a mutually agreeable outcome. But I have also made it much harder for myself to get upset over any outcome. Further, knowing that I have the power to deal constructively with my negative feelings seems surprisingly to diminish or even abort them from developing.

"Wow!" I thought: what a difference! Positive double binds on each side for both partners! By facing the negative feelings and finding a way to deal constructively with them, we are finessing them all around.

When I explained this to Larry, he was impressed. "Susan, hooray!" he said, "This is grass-roots leadership! Out of the box! How can I package this?"

"I will invite my Crone," I said, smiling.

"Crone?" he asked.

Oops. I decided then to keep all my dreams a secret. Then, thinking quickly, I said clearly, "I'll **recite** how I've **grown!**

"Oh," he said, "That's for sure."

Then, realizing how much I had learned and how freer I was, I laughed out loud and said, "Better still: I'll write a story and you can invite *me!*"

When we laughed together, I realized that it was the first time in a long time that we had both laughed at the same time.

The ground was lightly covered with snow yet winter scenes had for me the feeling that my world was now pregnant with possibility. Emily had turned 12 on November 29. Then, only a week ago, she came home from school and said she had discovered she really liked boys, not just because they both happened to like Harry Potter. I didn't panic. Believe it or not, I did not ask her whether it was a particular boy. I did not need to anticipate that.

Was that ever a change! Did I have a right to be proud of me? I knew the answer.

Win-Win Finesse Summary

When you have an issue with a working partner, that is, some behavior is getting in the way of working together well, possibly some negative feelings of which the other is unaware, decide to resolve this by the Win-Win Finesse method.

Remember this is an eye level, caring conversation so that tone of voice, demeanor, etc., is crucial, and that there are limitations.

The time and place for dealing with relationship issues should be in a place where the individual to whom your feedback is directed will not be distracted and where rapport can be more easily established. Consult the examples given for more illustration of how this is done.

Remember also that many people are typically unaware of their effect on others. Therefore, the feedback offered should not be accusatory in nature, but framed in such a way that it is understood that the feedback is given because you appreciate the relationship. To keep partnering strong and viable you must both understand how your words and actions affect others.

1. Say to the other, "Because I value our relationship (or your contributions to our team), I have something I need to talk with you about, but I am concerned that you may have negative feelings about it." Pause.

2. Once you have their attention, say, "And now may not be the best time." Pause. (In this qualification, you are asking for their consent at this time and inviting them to choose. The busy person may put you off, but not usually for long. If you are put off, get a luncheon date.)

3. After you have a "go ahead," tell them your concern and how the behavior causes difficulty for you. (If it is not obvious, you may need to explain how it is getting in the way of working well together, and why change is either useful and maybe even necessary. (These latter cases are usually safety issues or ongoing performance problems.)

4. Usually this will be enough. In some situations, for example, safety or ongoing performance issues, it may be necessary to talk further about the needed change of behavior.

Be aware of the limitations when it will not work:
A) with very task oriented, independent persons who pride themselves in getting to the point immediately;
B) with those who are suspicious of your motives;
C) probably not with teens; and
D) those few who are simply not open to any kind of confrontation.

Whenever possible, do this with food and beverage, e.g., over lunch. Remember practice makes perfect

For further information and updates, consult the many examples here of its use in further examples and see our web page www.winwinfinesse.com

Further Examples

These reports and those in the story are all real work/life experiences, applying Win-Win Finesse, reported in several Midway College School of Career Development evening courses, OM 313, Business Communication during the year 2003.

The reports are from non-traditional students in their 30s and 40s in a diversity of work environments. They have an average of 15-20 years in the workforce. Because the examples are by those who are learning to use the Win-Win Finesse on the job at their place of work, they are imperfect—sometimes the method is not used well and sometimes it does not work well. The reports have been edited occasionally for clarity. They are included here because of the learning demonstrated. That is, we do not have to do anything perfectly to change the present.

Moreover, they represent a wide diversity of work and home situations where this method can be applied. We do not know whether the requested changes were actually made, that is, whether the feedback "worked" down the road. The method does not guarantee change in behavior but the diplomatic reception of the change needed.

Persons and work situations are disguised. Students have graciously permitted their reports to be used here. Names of contributors are

Shannon Bailey
Barbara Baer
Gary Ball
Hubert Blanchard
Alean Burgess

Karen Chadwick
Prudence Daniell
David Faulkner
Lynn Forshee
Michael Hockensmith
Debra Darlene Hoover
Duane Lee
Clay McClure
Patricia Morris
Michael Pottinger
Brandon Ross
Jonathan Smith
Mark Smith
Donna Taylor
Eric Walz

List of Examples

Examples From Work

1. New manager with former co-worker
2. Confronting the boss
3. Taking personal calls effects work flow
4. Food makes feedback function freely
5. Confrontation is necessary for teamwork
6. Keeping my cool when interrupted
7. A put-off gets a luncheon invitation
8. Don't share my personal life with others
9. Make them a monitor of what they tend to do
10. Even explaining the Finesse may help others
11. This is nothing to get upset about
12. Confronting a domineering person
13. Saying no to my boss but keeping him happy
14. Your smoking in my office makes me ill
15. This negative reaction is not at all like you
16. Domineering persons keep interrupting
17. Complaining is "breakfast" for some
18. A special reason for my favorite parking space
19. Are you abusing your sick leave balance
20. Telling someone why they were not promoted
21. Effectively confronting a sensitive employee
22. Confronting associate performance
23. When Quality expectations become a pain

Examples From Personal and Family Life

24. A mother's preventive medicine
25. Because my sister is nuts...
26. How do I get "space" from my new girlfriend
27. My wife does not like my work hours

28. Apologizing in advance is preventive
29. Know-it-all types do not welcome feedback
30. No smoking, please, in my car
31. My sloppy careless husband
32. Getting my significant other to do chores
33. Does it really work on teenagers #1
34. Does it really work on teenagers #2

Examples From Work

Example 1. New manager with former co-worker
Context: Restaurant Management
Issue: Confrontation by a newly promoted manager

I attempted to use this method of conflict resolution twice with the same co-worker. I have recently been made a member of management. This former co-worker has a hard time accepting my new authority. I was not successful the first time but I did have moderate success the second time I attempted it.

The first occasion ended badly because I did not actually use the" Win-Win" method. I intended to, however when it came time to talk to the employee I became really uncomfortable and just said, "I am your boss, you have to do what I say."

Two days later I tried again. This time I followed the method very closely. When I said he might get upset, the employee thought I was giving him his notice but I assured him that that was not the case. When we sat down and talked I communicated the problems I was having with him. Then he told me about some fears and problems he was having which I was not aware of. I feel a lot better about working with him now. I also think he will feel better about his job. When we ended the discussion he thanked me for coming to him.

I feel I successfully applied the Win-Win method because the tension between the co-worker and myself was immediately relieved. However, I will not know if the conflict was truly resolved until a couple of weeks of normal working conditions have passed. This is why I feel I can only call my application of the Win-Win Method moderately successful at this time. (See example 10 for follow up on this example.)

Example 2. Confronting the boss
Context: Sales
Issue: Efficiency in team work

My third attempt at using the win-win conflict resolution method was more unnerving. Until this point I had used the method with employees under my control.

This attempt involved approaching my boss. Although the issue at hand was not a very big deal, it is still hard to approach someone of greater status than you. The problem was my boss had gotten into the habit of parking his vehicle in the back of our office. This seems simple, but actually creates some problems. For example his vehicle either blocks the bay door, or takes up a space where a truck is supposed to go. This also takes parking away from installers that work in the back of the building. My boss has no need to park there, and would be closer to his office if he came through the front. Because his truck is in the way, vehicles constantly have to be moved around when deliveries come in, or when we are loading a truck for a job. My goal was to get my boss to agree to park in the front of the building.

I approached the subject after a meeting that had already been scheduled. I started by saying I wanted to talk to him about something, but I was worried he would think I was being petty. He responded by saying he was sure I wouldn't bring it up if it wasn't worth mentioning. He went on to ask me what the problem was, and how he could help. I explained to him that I had noticed several instances where his vehicle had complicated some situations. After further explanation I asked him if it bothered him to park in the front.

In the end he assured me he had not thought about his being in the way, and agreed it would be simpler for him to avoid the back of the building.

Example 3. Taking personal calls effects work flow
Context: Construction business management
Issue: Personal Calls at work interrupting work flow

This past Tuesday I used the Win-Win conflict resolution technique for the first time. I had already identified a problem that needed addressing, so this method came at a convenient juncture. The problem was that one of my employees was taking phone calls at several intervals during the day. Many times he would drop what he was doing to answer a personal call. I wanted to find a way to persuade him to return his calls at lunch.

Under normal circumstances we talk about things while driving to a job site. On this occasion I waited until lunch so we could speak eye to eye. I started by telling him there was something we needed to go over, but I was worried it may hurt his feelings. He immediately responded by asking me to go over the problem. This made me more comfortable because it was obvious that he didn't want any problems to exist between us.

After determining the timing was right I very carefully laid out the problem for him. I explained that often his phone calls interrupted the process by which things are completed and ultimately costs additional time on the job. Next I presented him with a solution to the problem. I explained that because his phone has caller ID it would be easy to return his calls at lunch or during a break. This would avoid taking time from work.

His response was very positive. He said he didn't realize that he was creating a problem. He agreed to remember to take calls at times that didn't affect work. For the most part I simply had to make him aware of the problem so he could see it. I felt very good about solving the problem in this manner.

Example 4. Food makes feedback function freely

Context: Business Management, home remodeling.
Issue: Excessive tardiness affects team

I recently identified a second opportunity for using the win-win conflict resolution method. Based on its effectiveness the first time I used it, I had high expectations for resolving this conflict. The problem was that one installer in my team was excessively tardy. On average he was typically 15 minutes late, two or three days a week. This created problems because on many days the team is meeting a delivery driver, and the installers are late before they ever get started. Also they are often meeting a facility owner or a general contractor. It looks unprofessional when the team shows up at 8:30 when they were scheduled to be there at 8:00. This has happened several times when the employee in question showed up late. Even if the team is not on specific schedule, his being late means everyone else has to stay longer than they normally would have.

In solving this conflict I again chose to address the issue at lunch. I felt like it was a relaxed moment when it was easy to speak to him. The hardest part was finding a day when there would be no distractions. After we had finished eating, I said there was a problem, but that he probably would be offended. He countered by insisting I tell him what the issue was. From there I clearly explained the problem and its repercussions. He responded by saying he had no good reason for not being punctual.

Prior to our discussion he justified it by thinking as long as the job got done it all came out in the wash. We closed the discussion with him apologizing for his actions, and agreeing to correct them.

Example 5. Confrontation is necessary for teamwork
Context: Manufacturing coordination
Issue: Misunderstanding among shift leaders.

This last win-win strategy really happened to another person. They relayed the situation to me and I explained the win-win strategy to them and told them to try it.

John, a team leader on second shift, was told that his team had to cover overtime work for the coming weekend. He asked his team and was able to fill most of the slots. He still needed one more. He asked a lady whose husband is getting ready to go on strike on Friday, if she was interested. She had the skill and said yes, that they really needed the money.

Harry, the third shift team leader, got mad because the lady was not in our department. He wanted the overtime offered to our department first. In a very nasty manner Harry confronted John. Harry removed the woman's name from the overtime list and filled the slot with someone from his team. John felt like Harry overstepped his boundaries.

"Harry, I need to talk with you about the overtime for this weekend. You probably aren't going to like what I have to say. Is this a good time for you?"

Harry replied that he didn't think there was anything to talk about. He was just following departmental procedure. John explained to him that in the future he would post it first to the department. But he had an issue with Harry taking it on himself to remove the name and replacing it with someone from his own team.

"When it is my team's coverage, I do not want you to change a decision I have made without my permission. We need to work together as team leaders, not against one another. I also don't appreciate you confronting me in such a nasty manner. You could have approached me and discussed this with me in a civil manner, instead of jumping down my throat. Do you not think that would have been the more mature way to have handled this?"

Harry got a little embarrassed and said, "you are right, but I was tired from working third shift and it made me mad to have the overtime taken from my team. I will try and work on handling confrontations in a more mature way."

Example 6. Keeping my cool when interrupted
Context: Manufacturing supervisor and HRD
Issue: Supervisor not completing paper work creating extra work for others.

Hourly employees are able to bid or bump to other jobs in the production shop. Paperwork known as an EPCN is required for all personnel movement. Supervisors are to have their paperwork prepared by Friday so the employee will be listed on the appropriate supervisor's register the following Monday. We have a supervisor that periodically fails to do his paperwork until Monday. This causes us to be frantic until we get the employee's record keyed in the correct department. For the third week in a row, this supervisor did not prepare any EPCNs needed for the movement of the employees moving out of his group until Tuesday.

Payroll runs a week behind for hourly employees, so there is not a payroll issue. However, I have lost my patience with the supervisor not doing his job on time. That being said, I decided to approach the supervisor about the matter. I went to his office and asked him if he had a minute to talk to me. He welcomed me in and stated that it must be important if I walked out in the plant to see him. I informed him I wanted to talk to him about some paperwork missing on a few employees. We reviewed the list and got the information needed to finish our job.

I then stated I wanted to share some information that he might not like, but I felt it needed to be said. I informed him of the importance of getting the paperwork on time to Human Resources. When we do not get the paperwork, Monday becomes a rat race for us to try to complete work that was due on Friday. I began to share a few more facts with him.

However, the supervisor interrupted me over and over when I would be making my statements. I was able to maintain eye contact and control my voice. To shorten the story, we hashed out the situation whereby he understands clearly our position on the subject. He made a promise that he would have his paperwork in on time from now on. He explained he thought because payroll was a week behind, it didn't matter than he was a few days late. He stated that no one had ever spoken with him about being late, so he didn't think too much about it.

I walked away thinking I may have overstepped my authority. But I felt better about talking with him versus taking the problem up the chain of command. On the next Friday, the supervisor had employees moving out of his department. He completed his paperwork and sent me an e-mail stating he was "on top of it."

I had to smile when I received the e-mail, and I was very glad I had spoken with him.

Example 7. A put-off gets a luncheon invitation
Context: Commercial Accounts Dispatch
Issue: Getting time from a busy, overworked Dispatcher

We recently went through a "seat of the pants" job reorganization. Our dispatcher is now responsible for all scheduling except new construction. She has been given the responsibility of scheduling the commercial account maintenance customs. Here is brief highlight of a recent conversation concerning one of my commercial accounts. (Not the best way, but done over the phone since I am rarely in the office.)

Joe: "Hi Michelle, Randy with Acme Company just

called me about XYZ."

Michelle "I'll have someone out there as soon as I can. It's a little crazy right now."

Joe: "It is always crazy with service. Glad I am not doing it. Anyhow, I know you will get someone to see him soon. That's not all we talked about. He's concerned that he didn't get his walk-though in April or May. I want to see what we–

Michelle (interrupting) "He had his maintenance in April, and it's still May. What's his problem?"

Joe: "Michelle, I need to talk to you about something I'm concerned about. I'm afraid it might be taken negatively by you and right now may not be the best time to bring this up."

Michelle: "Whatever, it is, is going to have to wait. I have three lines on hold."

Joe: "Can I get you out of the office Friday? Buy you lunch and we will discuss it then."

Michelle: "Lunch would be appreciated. Friday is good!"

Joe: "We will talk on Friday then."

Michelle: "Tell Randy someone will be there within an hour."

This worked better than expected with someone who can be quite volatile.

———

Example 8. Don't share my personal life with others
Context: Business office, clients and friends.
Issue: Co-worker sharing too much personal information

Recently I have been having many family problems. My co-workers are aware of these personal issues and are sympathetic and accommodating. One of my co-workers is a secretary in the office pool and also a good friend. She has a tendency to divulge too much of my personal information to my clients or when I receive phone calls. I know she means no harm by this but I am a very private person. I do not like my personal matters being discussed by others.

Monday I received a call from a friend who had just spoken to this secretary. She asked me a personal question that no one else except my colleague could know. I was upset and decided this would be a perfect opportunity to use the Win-Win Finesse.

During break time, I asked my co-worker to go walking around the building with me. I know this is something she enjoys doing. While walking I told her how much I appreciate her friendship. There was something we needed to talk about, but I was concerned about her feelings.

When she seemed interested and wanted to hear more, I proceeded to tell how I was feeling about her giving so much information on my personal life to my clients and contacts. At first she seemed a little hurt, but then she apologized. She told me she did not realize she was being so liberal with information regarding me. She said she would change her actions and she should have been more aware of things she was discussing with business clients.

We later went to lunch together and nothing felt strained. I feel that this was a Win-Win situation.

Example 9. Make them a monitor of what they tend to do
Context: Organizational Meeting Effectiveness
Issue: Making a "chaser of rabbit trails" aware of their tendency.

People who go off on tangents, or rabbit trails here, there and everywhere, tend to prolong committee meetings. At work, on one committee I lead, John is a person who continuously goes off on tangents. I plan the agenda to keep the group focused on the issues at hand so we can easily get finished in a hour. I am usually well organized to get committee business done in the time limits we have.

In the past I have remarked when the discussion was going "off-track," but this did not seem to help. I realized that I needed to address this problem with John one on one.

I invited John to our conference room for a brief chat. We sat down next to each other. I told him I needed to talk with him, but was concerned that he might be offended. I also said that maybe this was not the best time for him. He asked me to continue.

First I told him how valuable he was to that particular committee, that he was one that I could always count on to speak up. I told him that he often had good ideas and a lot to offer. I was trying hard to make my feedback constructive.

I continued by saying, "However, you have a tendency to go off on tangents away from the agenda. This causes others to get off the agenda. I want to ask for your help to stay on the agenda. I explained the time constraints as well as the importance of staying focused during our meetings."

John first said that he was only trying to be helpful in the meeting. Then he asked me to make him aware of when he "went off." This would mean that I had to work harder and take responsibility for notifying him when it happened. This did not seem workable to me. We had a few awkward silences.

At this moment, I had a "brainstorm," a "what-if" of my own. After a pause, I decided to risk it. "John," I said, "I want you to be the one who notices when anyone goes off on tangents, and you have my permission to call out "Is this comment chasing rabbit tracks," or "...away from our agenda today?' "

Well, several weeks later, I cannot believe how well it is working. John really liked the idea. We have only had two meetings since, but the difference is amazing. John, by being alert to when others might go off track, simply does not do it anymore.

I felt this particular Win-Win Finesse was very effective, even though I added my "two bits." It encourages me to use it again.

Example 10. Even explaining the Finesse may help others

List of Examples

Context: Restaurant Business
Issue: Discipline by a new manager

Before beginning my report I would like to explain my situation. I am the sous chef of a small restaurant in Lexington. On a daily basis I interact with several cooks, one chef, one other sous chef, and several dish-washers.

We certainly have our communication problems and conflicts however I am not in a position to resolve them on my own. Last week the chef came to me and asked my advice on resolving a very large problem concerning the job performance of the other sous chef. She was in a "if I can't resolve this I will have to fire her" frame of mind. On a side note, the other sous chef is a friend of mine, she is a highly skilled cook but a shockingly bad manager. I described the win-win conflict resolution method to my boss and also suggested they have a meeting over lunch and described how this would change their dynamic and allow for a more open exchange.

I have always believed that you cannot sit at the same table with an enemy and eat a meal. You might chew your food but you will not notice taste. To enjoy a meal you have to relax and let your defenses down.

I realize that describing the win-win is not the same as practicing it. However I was able to stress the core concept of anticipating and changing the other's reaction through expressing concern for the other person's feelings, allowing the other person to have input on the time of the discussion and approaching the other person on an equal basis, without using any subtle power play.

So far my boss has not had a meeting with the sous chef however she has been looking at the nature of our kitchen communication as a whole to better understand the problem.

In reference to my previous win-win scenario, the employee seems to be happier and has changed his work habits. He now accepts criticism, asks for help or suggestions on his projects and takes directions from others. Now he lets us teach him what we know. Because of this his ideas and contributions seem to have more credence with the rest of us.

Example 11. This is nothing to get upset about
Context: Manufacturing
Issue: Overlooking safety rules

Our plant had just reached a plant safety record of 626 safe work days with no OSHA recordable injuries. We have safety rules that affect almost everything we do.

However, a male employee with an aggressive personality typically gets on the fork truck without filling out the fork truck inspection sheet. This is supposed to be filled out by the first person using the truck for the shift. When he placed the fork truck on the battery charger, he left the tines raised about three inches off the floor creating a trip hazard. They are supposed to be lowered all the way to the floor.

List of Examples

I approached the employee when he was alone at the computer station. I simply said, "I would like to speak with you about a safety issue that concerns me. It is nothing to get upset about. Is this a good time for you?" His eyes kind of darted around and he said, "Go ahead, shoot!"

I stated the safety outages and told him by following the safety rules he was keeping himself and others from possibly getting hurt. He said, "Are you sure it was me that left the tines up?" I told him the day and approximate time when he put the truck on the charger. He said, "I guess I was in a hurry." He tapped his ink pen on the table top the whole time. As he turned to go back to his computer work, he said, "Thanks for the 'heads up.'"

In our confrontation safety training at work, one is always supposed to thank someone if they confront them about safety.

Example 12. Confronting a domineering person regarding going behind my back
Context: HRD process
Issue: Complaint made directly to my boss regarding my handling of my job

ISSUE: An employee contacted my boss stating I had given her bad information regarding the 401k loan payoff procedures. The vendor holding the loan gave her information on how she could have paid off her loan and been able to obtain a new loan two weeks earlier than my procedures.

My boss shared the conversation he had with the employee. He was unaware of the process and wanted an explanation. I informed him of the standard procedure. I also explained that what the vendor told the employee could have happened, but we are to avoid making exceptions to the repayment agreement except in emergency situations.

After the above conversation, I went to the employee to discuss the matter further. I began by asking her if she had a few minutes to talk about her 401k repayment issue. I informed her it was not my intention to upset her, but I was informed she had some concerns, and I wanted to make sure she understood our company's administrative process. She stated she had a few minutes. I pulled my chair close to her desk, looked her in the eye and began to speak. I told her I was sorry she was not happy about the process I took for the repayment of her loan; however, I followed company procedures not the vendor's procedures. I continued to explain our process and why we did not follow the vendor's procedures. I also expressed my concern with employees not addressing their issues with me versus going to my boss, and I wanted to address that matter also. She agreed to talk further.

I maintained eye contact with her until she shifted in her seat and eye contact was not possible. The employee did interrupt me at times, but I maintained control of my voice when responding while hoping the employee would not turn hostile. She has a domineering personality and can get loud when she is angry. I concluded the conversation by asking if she had any questions still needing answering about her loan repayment or any other benefit issues. She indicated she didn't and apologized for going to my boss versus talking with me. She said she would speak with me first about the benefit issues in the future.

Example 13. Saying no to my boss but keeping him happy
Context: School administration, private academy
Issue: When ambition clashes with status quo.

My position as Assistant to the Headmaster at The Learning Academy is about to change dramatically. Our current Headmaster is leaving to assume a position at another school. Allowing the school to conduct a proper search for a new Head of School, the Board of Trustees has hired an interim head for the next school year.

Knowing I am interested in another open position in the school, the Interim Head has asked for me to consider greatly staying in my current position, allowing him consistency and support during his year at the school. I sat down with him today to discuss my interests in the other position and my desire for such professional growth.

As we sat down to talk, I made sure that I was not sitting any higher than he was sitting. I told him that I wanted to talk about my interests in the other position available at The Learning Academy, but was concerned about how he would take it. I did not want to upset him or make him think that I do not want to work for him. I am simply at a stage professionally where I am ready to grow within the organization, without having to look outside this academy for advancement. I told him that I understand his need for support and consistency in the transition. But I also explained that I could serve the Academy and his administration better in the new position now open.

The Interim Head did not get upset about our conversation. He listened well to everything I had to say. He said that he would consider my suggestions for alternate arrangements that would allow me to move into another position, but still allow him the stability he desired for his year of serving the Academy.

Example 14. Your smoking in my office makes me ill
Context: Government agency
Issue: My right to a smoke free environment in my own office

The organization I work for is an agricultural agency, which is a strong promoter of tobacco products. The company is probably one of the only government agencies which still allows smoking in the building. I am the only employee who does not smoke and I do not have a problem with anyone who does, but one of my co-workers comes into my office every morning to smoke and drink her morning coffee. I enjoy her company but the stench of her cigarette lingers in my office and makes me physically ill.

Last Friday morning while my co-worker was in my office, I thought I would try the win-win solution her. When she came into my office for her morning ritual I asked her if she had time to sit down so we could talk. She did. I then proceeded to tell her that I enjoyed our morning talks but there was something that I wanted to ask her. She looked at me with concern as I assured her of our friendship.

I said "I hope you do not take this the wrong way or become angry with me, but it is that you smoke in my office. I know you didn't know it but the smell of cigarettes truly makes me ill. I really want you to come visit me in the morning but, could you smoke before or after you visit?"

I felt a little strange making the request but my co-worker just simply said "Why didn't you tell me? I would have never brought my cigarettes around you if I knew it made you ill. It's a nasty habit anyway!"

This approach worked nicely in this situation. She doesn't smoke in my office and has actually cut down on her consumption of cigarettes.

Example 15. This negative reaction is not at all like you
Context: Banking and collections
Issue: Customer service

Martha came into the computer room at 4:40 p.m. looking for the Customer Service Supervisor, who was in a meeting. She said another supervisor had just let in an elderly man but the tellers had already closed up and would not take his money.

I walked out to the teller's window and first asked Grace if they could open their batch and take the money. She said that Sally, head teller, had already written everything up. I then asked Sally if she could take the money and rewrite the teller's report. Sally then said, in a loud voice, with the customer just outside her window:

"Ann let him in and I am not taking any money. If she wants to take it, let her take it. I've got to go to class, I am not taking any money."

I then walked into the lobby and spoke with the gentleman and asked if he needed change. His bill was $19.37 and he had a $20 bill. He said "No, just subtract it from my next bill." I took the $20 and will process it on the next day.

While I understand Sally's reason for not taking the money due to policies, I thought she should have been more discreet about the situation. She could have asked Ann to take the money and pay the bill for Mr. Smith tomorrow.

The next day, I asked Sally to come into my office when she had a chance. I have two chairs in my office and I sat in the chair next to Sally and began the conversation.

"Sally, I was worried about you last night. Are you OK? Can you talk about this now?"

She said "I'm fine, I just had a stressful day yesterday and I was in a hurry to get to my class."

I said "I know that was not like you and I was concerned. I understand why you didn't want to take the money, but I thought you should have been more polite to the customer. I am sure he now has an impression about us that is not true.

Sally said "Sue, that is not the first time Ann has let in customers after hours. It creates a real security issue for us, with our money spread out everywhere. I felt really bad for the gentleman and I know I should not have acted that way. I thought you were going to suspend me."

I told Sally that I knew that was not her normal personality and was sure it would not happen again. I also told her I would talk to Ann about admitting customers after hours.

I felt good about the conversation with Sally. I thought that she understood 1) I was concerned for her, but also 2) that type of behavior would not be tolerated in the future. She was very apologetic and I feel we really connected during this conversation.

Example 16. Domineering persons keep interrupting
Context: Business management
Issue: Co-worker who constantly interrupts me when I am speaking to others.

I stopped by my co-worker's office. I asked my co-worker if we could talk about an issue I was having with some of the employees. She welcomed me and said she would be glad to help me if she could. I proceeded to tell her how some employees will interrupt me when I am speaking with other employees regarding benefits or other matters. She said she was guilty of that as well. I confirmed her admission and stated I wanted to talk about that also without hurting her feelings. She agreed.

I proceeded to explain how important having control of the conversation is when helping an angry employee. I emphasized when another party gets involved in the conversation, it allows the employee to take additional time to vent. Then the employee can become even more agitated. The result is that the employee is away from their duties longer than necessary.

At this point she became a little defensive. I told her it was not my intent to anger her or hurt her feelings, but I felt I needed to address this situation. I tried to maintain eye contact throughout the conversation.

I continued my conversation until we came to an agreement. The result is my co-worker agreed not to get involved in my conversation with employees in the future.

Example 17. Complaining is "breakfast" for some
Context: Office politics
Issue: A co-worker who is a friend dumps on me regularly about her supervisor
Isabel is a co-worker who is also a dear friend. Lately,

she has gotten into the habit of coming into my office, as well as that of other employees, each morning and venting about her supervisor. This has become a very negative start to my workday and I have found myself avoiding any contact with her. I see others reacting to her the same way. Since she is also a friend I felt it would be better to address this issue with her instead of ignoring her.

I asked her to lunch on a recent Monday, which pleased her very much. I said there was something I wished to discuss with her but that it was an uncomfortable issue for me. I proceeded to tell her what a dear friend she was. Then I explained that her behavior I observed recently was disturbing to me. When she begins the day by communicating such negative and redundant feelings each morning, that was not a good way to start her day or mine. She was, at first, somewhat surprised that I felt this way, but was very understanding of my feelings.

Isabel then told me what an inspiration I was to her and was very apologetic regarding her behavior and attitude change. She said she appreciated my being up front with her and knew that I was only looking out for her well being.

I must say this is a big relief for me!

Example 18. A special reason for my favorite parking space
Context: Personal and family relations

Issue: My parking space is reasonably special

I have finally gotten the nerve to try this strategy at work. I chose a co-worker that I have a good relationship with to practice on. The issue was very minor, almost comical. The following is the result of this experiment:

ME: "Jeannie, we need to talk, but I do not want you to get upset."
JEANNIE: "Why would I get upset? You know we can talk about anything. What is it?"
ME: "Well, OK! I've noticed that lately you've been parking in my favorite space.   I know you know I like to park there, so I feel like you are doing this on purpose. What is going on?
JEANNIE: "I didn't know you had a favorite space!"
ME: "Yes I do. I park there because I can see my car when I am inside the building and also because when I leave in the evenings, I can get to my car quickly. This helps me when I work late. I can look outside before I leave to be sure there is not anything or anyone suspicious out there before I leave the building. I park there more for security purposes than convenience. "
JEANNIE: "Well I didn't know that. You should have told me sooner! I will park in the next space from now on."
ME: "Thank you for being so understanding.

Example 19. Are you abusing your sick leave balance
Context: Handling Put-downs by one's manager.
Issue: Implications that I am mis-using my sick leave.

List of Examples

I used the Win-Win Finesse method with a recent comment made by my branch manager. She stated to me, "you do know that your sick leave balance is getting low, and just what did you go to the doctor for?" Zappo!

Her words not only struck a nerve but it was the tone in which she said it. I did not respond at that moment as I was shocked and speechless.

Later, I did take the opportunity to approach her alone in the break room. I honestly and simply stated that I value our professional and personal friendship. But that I have something I need to talk about, but that I am concerned that she might not like and be upset. As this was in the break room, I explained to her this may not be the best time, so we could meet later, either in the cafeteria or outside at the picnic table.

When my manager said that now is a good time, I began explaining how I interpreted her recent comment. What she said left me thinking that I had done some wrong. Or maybe she felt I was abusing my sick leave. This was the reason I have been upset and avoiding her.

To my relief, she apologized and explained that she was also having a particularly bad day. Also, she was sorry that she had not stopped to consider how she spoke. She explained that she was truly concerned about my health and how another hospital stay could drain all my leave balances. We parted both feeling better understanding as we both shared the same concerns.

Example 20. Telling someone why they were not promoted
Context: Non-promotion in an ambulance service.
Issue: Valuable employee passed over for promotion

I am the director for a municipal ambulance service. We have thirty full-time, and about half that number part-time employees. Recently, we promoted a person to the position of supervisor. Another employee was very upset that he was not chosen for the position. This employee does possess all the requirements and has more seniority. In addition, the employee has more education than me or any of us.

However, his problem is that he is not a team player, and does not interact well with his co-workers. The employee has been standoffish towards me since the promotion. In the past, I have tried to talk with the individual but with little success in changing his attitude and demeanor. So, I tried the Win-Win Finesse method.

When the employee was in the office, I asked him to come to the conference room to talk to me. I also let him know up front, that he was not in any trouble, and I have not received a complaint against him. I chose the conference room because it is casual and should not be an intimidating setting. On sitting down I addressed him, " Joe, because I value your years of experience, and contributions to the service, I need to talk to you about something, but I am concerned that you may

already have negative feelings about it. (Pause) However, now maybe is not the best time."
It did not take a lot of time for his response. He thought for just a moment, and informed me nonchalantly "Now's as good a time as any."

I explained the situation that he is an excellent para-medic, and more than qualified for any position that we have. However, his attitude and demeanor have pre-vented his being promoted. I explained that being a good supervisor takes more than just knowledge. It takes a person who can listen, understand co-workers feelings, integrate well with others and only when needed gets involved in disciplining personnel. I also explained to him that if he would attempt to change his attitude that I would entrust him with more responsi-bility and highly consider him for the next promotion.

Although I am not sure that he entirely believed me, he did not respond negatively and stated that he would appreciate that. Since he has over ten years service in with the company, he did not wish to leave, but did not want to stay stagnant. I again assured him that I har-bored no ill feelings towards him. I did value his past contributions, and would like to see him succeed in the organization. We parted friendly.

———

Example 21. Effectively confronting a sensitive employee
Context: Getting Agreement after Needed Confrontation
Issue: Does this work with someone who is easily hurt?

I attempted the Win-Win strategy on one of my employees. This particular employee is one that I see and deal with on a daily basis. He is very sensitive and gets his feelings hurt easily. I felt this strategy would work well for him.

The situation that I wanted to discuss with him was the problem he was having in prioritizing tasks that were to be completed. I began the conversation with both of us in the maintenance shop. This is an area where we routinely have discussions on various subjects other than work related items. I told him that I needed to talk to him about something that was bothering me and that I did not want to hurt his feelings. But I thought that this was something that needed to be addressed. I then allowed him the option of bowing out of the conversation by telling him that if this was not a good time for him that we could continue this at another time.

He wanted to discuss the problem, so I continued. Next, I expressed my concern about how he prioritized projects and tasks. I explained to him that there were some tasks that must be completed before others depending on the situation. He could not just simply get into a routine of doing the same projects in the same manner each day. Some things arose that must be dealt with immediately. Sorting what is urgent from what is not immediate is where he needed improvement.

I then offered my assistance that whenever he was not clear about a situation, he could ask for my help. But I also told him that I wanted him eventually to learn to sort the differences himself and be able to handle these situations as they arise.

I again expressed my concern of his feelings by telling him that I hope that he was not offended by the things that I had said and invited him to respond to these items. He agreed that he needed improvement in this area. He wanted me to speak up whenever I noticed something that was not in order.

The strategy worked well, I accomplished my goal and got a positive response from the employee.

Example 22. Confronting associate performance
Context: Emergency medical service delivery
Issue: Getting associate to accept feedback

As an Emergency Medical Service supervisor, I noticed in reviewing reports a cardiac arrest run report. Medication delivery times were a little askew. I asked the paramedic involved to come to my office to talk. I let him know that he was not in any trouble. We sat in chairs in front of my desk. I then said, " Jason, because I value your years of experience and contributions to the service, I need to talk to you about something. But I'm concerned that you may have negative feelings about it." I then paused. When I got no reaction, I continued, "However, now may not be the best time." Before I could say anything else, he stated, "It's Okay, I know I screwed up on that code last time. I just wasn't as comfortable without James (his regular partner)." I asked how he'd screwed up. He said he realized, after he had documented the run, that he should have given the epinephrine at shorter intervals. He said that he depends on his regular partner who is also a paramedic. They remind each other when to administer medications. He realized this was no excuse, but this was the first cardiac arrest he had worked as the only paramedic on the scene. He went on to say that he would be more diligent in the future.

I told him I appreciated his honest assessment of the call and that I had every confidence in him as a paramedic. I assured him his actions were not deleterious to the patient, and that we all overlook things from time to time. As long as we learn from our mistakes and do not repeat them, that is all that we can ask.

By my pausing, I believe the employee was able to address my concerns before I even had to bring it up. This also allowed me to realize that the employee is doing a self-assessment. I know that he cares about his performance and will always improve.

———————

Example 23. When quality expectations become a pain
Context: Cooperation with Quality Control in production
Issue: Getting line help with a quality control issue

This week I had the opportunity to practice the win-win method with a production supervisor in large parts production. The general attitude there is that Quality Department is considered the police department in the plant and that they are the ones responsible for parts quality.

My conversation started "George, do you have a few minutes so that we can talk about customer expecta- tions and the daily issues we are seeing? If this is not a good time I can come back later."

Normally I would just tell him what was happening and go away to look at other things as he mumbled that the customer quality expectations are constantly changing but that he would do whatever I told him.

George said that since I was there and since Quality usually gets their way, he had to take time to talk to me. I said that he did not have to take time for me if he was busy but I needed his help solving a quality issue some time today. We ended arranging a meeting among Quality, Production and Tooling for 3:00 p.m. to review the issue and look for solutions.

The tooling supervisor opened a tool in the shop and carried the part with the concern to the meeting for the problem-solving. Generally this type of condition is acceptable to the customer but there have been ques- tions of the acceptable amount. I thought that if we got rid of the issue, the questions would go away. While reviewing the issue, several solutions were discussed from pencil vents, auto vents, and maybe blending a radius to allow more consistent chemical flow. Finally we settled on blending the radius better and polishing and area of the tool to make it deeper, the first tool was done then and put back into production and when the part was run the problem had gone away. We proceed- ed to rework all remaining tools which completely fixed the issue stopping the need for questions.

George thanked me. I thanked him and the tooling supervisor for their help. George walked away saying that we should do this sort of thing more often to make it easier for production to eliminate guess work.

This ended better than the normal approach because most people approach him, tell him what they think needs to happen and then expect him to get the rest of the team to do what they are told—instead of getting his opinion while using a team approach to come up with a better solution.

Examples From Personal and Family Life

Example 24. A mother's preventive medicine
Context: Personal and family relations.
Issue: Wife confronting husband

Although I have already explained the Win-Win strategy to my husband, I wanted to see how the approach would work with him. My husband sometimes gets so caught up in his schedule that he can often forget the need to take special time with our daughter. I decided the Win- Win approach would allow me to address this issue without him getting upset with me.

It was a quiet evening, after our daughter had gone to bed. I sat down across the couch from Paul and told him that I wanted to talk to him about something that I felt was very important and had been concerning me. I asked him if, although it had been a long busy day, would be ok for us to talk. I told him that I was not sure how he would feel about what I had to say, that I did not want to come across as attacking him or criticizing him as a parent because I feel he is a wonderful husband and father, but that I thought that Ally needed more attention from him.

Paul and I then discussed the relationship he has with our daughter and the need for them to have their own special connection. I told him that I felt it was important for her to see that he would set things aside every once in a while so that they could have quality time together.

Paul expressed some of his hesitations of not always knowing what to do with her since he grew up with a brother. He said that he still sometimes feels like he doesn't know how to connect with a little girl. I assured him that they could find a mutual interest on which to build a relationship. I also suggested that he take the opportunity to pick her up from school every so often and take her out to dinner, just the two of them. This would give them the opportunity to talk. Paul was very open to this discussion and the suggestions. I think their relationship will grow from this discussion.

Example 25. Because my sister is nuts about house-keeping
Context: Personal and family situations.
Issue: Two sisters at odds and I am in between

This is a personal issue between two of my sisters. My older sister, Jeanette, complained to me, yet again, about one of my younger sisters, Norma. Norma always invites people over to Jeanette's house without her permission. Jeanette is very picky about her house and if anyone other than family is coming over she requires a week's notice. When my younger sister brings someone unannounced, she gets very upset.

It has been this way for years. We have never understood how Norma has not adjusted to this. On Memorial Day, Norma invited Harriet to Jeanette's house for the cookout. Jeanette called me and let off all her steam about how mad she was. How she was having to do rush around doing cleaning she would not have normally done. I told her I would try the Win-Win Strategy.

I met Norma over at her place before the cookout. I asked her if I could speak to her for a few minutes about a personal problem that affected our family and would probably upset her. She said, "What could it be?"

I explained the whole scenario of how "unreasonably upset" Jeanette becomes when an unannounced guest arrives. Even though it doesn't bother us if her house is not spotless, it bothers her very much. It is her house. I explained that it was part of Jeanette's personality and at this point, she cannot help being so finicky about her home's cleanliness.
"Since it upsets her so much," I said, "would you please not invite an extra guest to family gatherings at her house?

She responded that Jeanette must have called me. She

said it didn't matter because Harriet could not come anyway. I told her that it was not just for this incident, this was from now on. I told her that Jeanette may need to get help to overcome this need to have her house spotless. She was very quiet and finally just said, "all right."

The rest of the day Norma was in a somber mood. Everyone wondered why she was not very social. The test will be to see if she slips and invites someone without giving Jeanette a week's notice.

Example 26. How do I get "space" from my new girlfriend
Context: Interpersonal relationships
Issue: Negotiating time available for closeness

The win/win finesse conflict resolution provided me with a way to deal with particular concerns that I had with a romantic relationship. This week I needed to tell my new girlfriend that I needed a little space. We see each other three to four days a week, have lengthy phone conversations on the days we do not meet, and e-mail several times daily.

Only six months ago, I broke off contact with someone that I had been dating for several years. Although I was not interested in beginning a new relationship, I was so impressed with my first encounter with my new girlfriend that I could not help but pursue her. We have now been dating a couple months, and even though I care for her deeply, I feel like I need a little more space.

I began by expressing her value to me, and assuring her that I was honored to have her company. I then told her I had something to tell her that may affect the way she felt about our relationship. She expressed some concern at this point, and I said that maybe this was not the best time for us to have this conversation. She compelled me to continue. I told her that due to what had happened in my previous relationship, and the fact that it had so recently ended I felt like I needed more space to deal with my feelings.

I said that this in no way reflected on her and that I was crazy about her. I think that after the build up, she was pleasantly surprised that it was only a little more time to myself that I needed. She assured me that our relationship was important to her, and she would do whatever it took to ensure its health.

Needless to say, I was pleased at this outcome.

Example 27. My wife does not like my work hours
Context: Interpersonal Relationships
Issue: How to keep my spouse from getting upset

I work a lot of hours and my wife doesn't like it. We enjoy being together and when I have to work Saturdays she gets upset. Because I want to avoid facing her upset, I usually wait until the last minute to let her know that I am working extra hours. Sometimes I tell her on Friday morning or sometimes-over dinner on Friday night. To say the least this can ruin an evening together.

List of Examples

After class I tried the Win-Win strategy on my wife. As soon as I heard about the strategy I knew who I would try it on first. I went in the house after class and she was watching television. We talked about our day at work. I told her about class. She was very interested in the television show so we only talked during commercials and when I thought it was a good time.

Then–I think it was during the third or fourth commercial—I said, "Honey I love you very much and I have something I need to talk with you about, but it is not all that important."
She answered, "What is it."
I said. "Don't worry about it we can talk about it later."
She turned off the television immediately, and said. "No, tell me now."
I said. "Go ahead and watch your show. It can wait till the show goes off."
She said. "No, lets talk now."

I went on to explain since we have an audit coming up in a few weeks at work, I am going to traveling to France on business within the month. Furthermore, school is taking more time than I expected. I explained to her that I really needed to work this coming weekend and possibly the following weekend.
Believe it or not, she said "OK". She asks if there was anything she could do to help. She said she will probably go to work with me this weekend and do some filing.

We love being together and this worked out great. This is one of the few times we have not argued over me working on weekends.

Example 28. Apologizing in advance is preventive
Context: Personal, husband and wife.
Issue: Husband forgetting a gift for Mother's day

I used the win-win solution to approach my wife about the lack of a Mother's Day gift from me. I approached her while working together in the kitchen preparing for the installation of our new cabinets. I began to address the issue while standing together scraping wallpaper off the wall.

In hindsight, with her having a sharp object in her hand might have had a negative outcome for me had this not worked. Anyway, the conversation went something like this:

Joe: (While looking into her eyes) "I need to talk to you about something I am concerned about, but I am afraid you might take it personally!"
Jean: OK
Joe: "Now might not be the best time to bring this up."
Jean: "It's just the two of us right now. Seems like as good a time as any."
Joe: "I don't have a thing for you for Mother's Day, not even a card."
Jean: "Don't worry about it. We are getting a new kitchen aren't we? Besides, I am not your mother now am I? Besides, I didn't get you anything for our anniversary, not even a card!"

Boy, do I feel lucky. It was a lot easier bringing it up at the time and place of my choosing, rather than the next morning when I would have been expected to deliver.

Example 29. Know-it-all types do not welcome feedback
Context: Personal and family relationships
Issue: Bossy unmarried sister frequently corrects our children

I have several sisters and brothers, and three of us have children ranging from 17 years old down to nine years old. One of my sisters has never been married, has no children, yet she is judgmental and openly critical of the rest of us. Over the years we have all put up with her jumping in and correcting our children. This happens even when we are already in the act of correcting them or preparing to do so. Sometimes, she gets very nasty and overly loud while doing this. It is embarrassing for all who witness this. We feel it is our responsibility to correct our children without her assistance. .

Recently she was at my house in the living room watching television. I walked in and said, "Kathy, I would like to talk to you about something that has been bothering me for years. This may make you uncomfortable or upset. May we discuss this now?" She asked me, "What is it?"

I described to her how many times over the years she had taken it on herself to correct all our children unnecessarily. I explained that I was talking about times when the adults were present and were either already reprimanding our kids or getting ready to. I told her how uncomfortable it made everyone feel when she would get so mean and nasty with the nieces and nephews, even when we were already addressing the problem.

She looked a little uncomfortable, and said it rarely happened. She added that we should appreciate her helping and, furthermore, it didn't hurt kids to hear it twice.

I didn't want to argue with her, so I closed with, "In the future, we would appreciate it if you would let us handle the discipline if we are around."

Even if nothing in her behavior changes, I know it made me feel really good to speak my mind. I am anxious to see what happens the next time the situation arises.

Example 30. No smoking, please, in my car
Context: Personal and family relations
Issue: Smoke free environment.

I tried the win-win technique on my sister, Ella, who has a disregard for other people's right to be in a smoke free environment.
We were headed to the store to pick-up a few things for a cookout we were having at our mother's house when she rolled down her window and pulled out a pack of cigarettes. Normally, I would have ranted and raved over the fact that she was smoking.

But this time I opted to have a discussion with her about smoking in my car. I began with "Ella, I would like to talk to you about something, but you may not like what I am going say or ask of you." She looked at me with a puzzled face and said "What?"

I said "Well, I do not mean to hurt your feelings but I would appreciate it if you would not smoke while you are in my car. It bothers my eyes and leaves a film on the windows. So, if you would not mind, and please do not be offended but would you please not smoke while we are riding together?"

My sister looked at me, put her cigarettes away, closed her purse up and said, "That's fine, sorry!"

I am very impressed with this technique! I will keep using it until I find someone it doesn't work on.

Example 31. My sloppy careless husband
Context: Personal and family relations
Issue: Getting my husband to pick up after himself

I am a little reluctant to use this tool in my workplace, so I've started my experiments with my husband. The following is the result of my first attempt to use the Win-Win strategy.

A minor issue with my husband concerns how he handles his dirty laundry. As I am the one who does the laundry, I have asked him simply to place his dirty clothes in the appropriate laundry baskets, instead of leaving them on the closet or bathroom floor. No matter how many times I have asked and reminded him, he still does not use the baskets. I approached him one evening after dinner to discuss this issue. Using the principles of the Win-Win strategy, I began the conversation as such:

ME: "There is something I want to talk to you about, but I do not know how you are going to respond, and the last thing I want to do is upset you."

HIM: "Is it that serious?"

ME: "To me, it is."

HIM: "Well, let's talk about it. I promise I will not get upset."

ME: "It's about the laundry. I've asked you several times to use the baskets I bought, but you still leave your laundry on the floor every night. When you do this, it makes me feel like you do not care about my feelings. I ask you to use the baskets because it makes it easier for me to do the laundry."

HIM: "I never even pay attention to the laundry. I didn't know you felt this way. From now on, I will do my best to put my dirty clothes where they belong. Thanks for telling me this."

Example 32. Getting my significant other to do chores
Context: Interpersonal relationship
Issue: Can my boyfriend do chores without being asked?
I sat down with my significant other and said to him, "I learned a new technique in class on Monday." I explained to him how it worked. We were on the couch. I looked him in the eye and said, "I want you to know that I value this relationship very much. I need to talk to you about something that you may not like. I don't want you to feel like it is anything negative but I am concerned you might think it is."

Than I told him that I was not sure now was the best time. I said if you would rather I come back later, I will do that. He said it was a good time.

I told him that I wished that when he came over to visit, that he would feel comfortable enough to take my garbage out or wash a few dishes, or if he saw something that needed to be done, that he would just do it without me having to ask him. He said OK.

The next day when I came in, I saw that he had put the mini blinds up in the kitchen. He had also taken out the trash. When I said, "Thank you," he said that he had really appreciated the way that I approached him and that he was much more receptive to do what I asked him to do than if I had just nagged or hinted or complained.

I was pleased and surprised that this worked so well.

———

Example 33. Does it really work on teenagers #1
Context: Personal and family relations
Issue: My son–the class clown
My 18-year-old son, Rudy, has great talent for irritating me beyond belief. For some reason, he thinks that behaving like a "class clown" will predispose me to say yes to whatever he wants at the time. I know Dr. B said the "Win-Win" strategy may not work on teenagers, but I tried anyway. The following is the result of this experiment:
ME: "Rudy I really need to talk to you about something that has been bothering me, but I am not sure how you

are going to feel about it."

RUDY: "What is it? What have I done?"

ME: "You have not done anything. It's more about how you do things."

RUDY: "I do not understand, but I promise I will not be upset. What is it?"

ME: "Every time you need or want something, you always play around and make jokes instead of just asking. It's like you think that if you can just make me laugh, I will give you whatever it is you want. This makes me feel like you are always trying to get something past me, so I am more likely to say no to whatever it is you want. Next time you want something, just ask me. I will appreciate it and will be more receptive to what it is you want if you treat me with the same respect.

RUDY: "I thought you liked my jokes! I am just trying to put you in a good mood before I ask."

ME: "I understand that, but I think we are at a point where we can deal with each other like adults. Why don't we try it for a while and see what happens."

RUDY: "I'm willing, if you are, but you are going to miss out on some great jokes!"

ME: "Well, I am willing to take that chance!"

RUDY: "You mean you don't want to laugh, Mom?"

ME: "No, I do not want to feel like I am being conned."

RUDY: "Okay, but you will miss my practice in becoming a great comedian."

ME: Walked away laughing. Maybe he is right.

Example 34. Does it really work on teenagers #2

Context: Can a divorced mom date?

List of Examples

Issue: Permission from my daughter

This is funny, because I proved it did work with teenagers.

A few weeks ago, a gentleman at my church asked me out to dinner. I was interested in going but hesitated to tell my daughter because the last time I went out with anyone she seemed to want to sabotage it. It has been less than two years since I got out of an abusive marriage that lasted only seven months and she has never wanted me to date.

But I made up my mind–she is 15 and I am 41 years old. I am not going to go out with anyone or everyone but I would say "yes" if I felt strongly enough about this person after I got to know him some first. So I decided to tell her. Here is how the conversation went.

Me: "Tiffany..."

Tiffany: "Yes?"

Me: "I need to talk with you about something I am not sure you are going to like. I am afraid it might upset you, and I love you and do not want to see you upset. So, if this is not a good time...."

Tiffany: "What is it? I know you are going to gripe at me about bickering with Jane (her friend), and how I need to be nicer."

Me: "No, honey, not at all."

Tiffany: "Then what? Are you mad at me for something else? Just tell me."

Me: "Well, I met a gentleman at church about four weeks ago and he seems really nice. He has asked me to go out to dinner and I want to go. But I do not want

to have you upset at me."
Tiffany: "Oh Mom! That is great. No, I want you to go.
I want you to have some fun. Mom, what is he like?"
Totally not what I expected. It worked. I am definitely
going to use this method again.

Afterword

The Win-Win Finesse gives us for the first time a positive way to defuse negative feelings in advance, by a simple yet subtle and open way that begins with valuing the relationship. The hidden effect is that not only invite the other to defuse their own negative reaction, but we also defuse our own feelings. We create a new sense of the ability to work together anywhere despite differences in views, temperament and backgrounds. We actually create a new climate for openness and bonding when we do this.

No one has ever suggested that an employee might face a supervisor or a boss with negative feelings about that person's behavior with a positive outcome. We offer that this Win-Win Finesse has as many applications as there are differing persons working and living together

If you believe that the Win-Win Finesse is an idea and a method "whose time has come," and would like to help promote this method in the workplace, family and home, church or wherever people gather to talk, plan and work together, to increase openness, mutuality and bonding, you may wish to visit our web page at www.winwinfinesse. You are invited to discuss your experience and your use of this method with others. We also invite you to post examples from your own use of the Win-Win Finesse for discussion online.

We want you to tell us your story, share your examples and challenges, and have fun promoting a climate of caring mutuality wherever you are. Participants are dedicated to the principles outlined here to promote the tradition of caring confrontation in the workplace, the family and the world.

A Win-Win Finesse Workbook and Facilitators

Handbook is being developed. This is a Discussion Guide and Tips for the Facilitator to help lead discussions on the use of this method in various organizations and companies.

For those who want to learn to teach this method to others, training and newsletters will be available. Register your email address with Paschal at paschal@winwinfinesse.com You will be sent an application blank.

Please visit our web page in progress:
www.winwinfinesse.com

About the Author

Paschal Bernard Baute is an organizational psychologist who has been a consultant to more than 50 companies and organizations for over 30 years. He has designed training and leadership assessment programs and also coached and mentored numerous executives and managers. Corporate clients include banks, manufacturing, service industries, law and architecture firms, engineering and electronic firms, sales organizations, city government, military, churches, fire and police departments, construction firms, public schools, and nonprofit organizations.

He has published The Complete Counselor Tool Kit along with more than 200 handouts for human resource managers, trainers and consultants. He has designed and led many workshops in conflict resolution in diverse settings. He has written a manuscript, Hidden Lions, on the ways that managers and leaders undermine their career success. He is widely known as an effective trainer and presenter. At the University of Kentucky he taught a variety of courses in psychology. Currently, he teaches Business Communication and Leadership courses in the School for Career Development at Midway College, Midway, Ky.

His career has spanned the fields of the military, coaching sports, ministry, educational administration, psychotherapy, marriage and family therapy, and consulting and training applying psychology to the work place. He has served with several branches of the U.S. military, active and reserve, enlisted and commissioned. He has a rich and diverse background for understanding human relations and organizational dynamics. He has completed and published original research in several fields including marital intimacy, pastoral counseling, psychological assessment, spirituality and forensics.

He has Bachelor's degrees from St. Benedict College and the University of Notre Dame. He earned a Master's degree in Psychology from Loyola University of Chicago and a doctorate in Educational Psychology and Counseling from the University of Pennsylvania. He is a member of Division 14, the Society for Industrial and Organizational Psychology of the American Psychological Association.

He has been listed in the regional *Who's Who–Life in the Bluegrass,* by J. Winston Coleman. He is married to Janette Osborne Mobley for 35 years, and they have three children and three grandchildren. The family has been active in water skiing, horseback riding and downhill skiing.

His business web site is found at:
www.paschalbaute.com

*Discuss this book with your partner,
teammates, work group, book club
or lunch group at work*

Win-Win Finesse Guidebook for Discussion Leaders

*Contents
Questions for Discussion on each chapter
Twenty suggestions for the leader to
help maximize discussion
Ten guidelines for club or group*

plus

*NEW MATERIAL ON
Listening, Managing Conflict, Conflict-Avoidance,
Anger, Types of People this will not work with,
How to Understand Your Own Communication
Style, etc.
Sixty pages*

© Paschal Bernard Baute, 2003
Price $5.95 each

Order Form for Consumers (1-5 copies)

SEND TO (PLEASE PRINT)
Name _____

Address _____

City _____State _____

Zip_____Email or Phone _____

WWF book price $12.95 each. WWF Leaders Guide price $5.95 each. Postage and handling for one book (US/Can) $2.50, or $4.00 priority mail; add $1.00 for each additional book. We accept checks or money order. No cash/COD. Special bulk discount for organizations. Inquire Email paschal@winwinfinesse.com. This offer is subject to change without notice. $20.00 fee for returned checks.

Send your order to:
BAUTE PUBLICATIONS
4080 LOFGREN COURT
LEXINGTON, KY 40509-9520

ORDER

_____ copies of WWF book @ $12.95 each $ _____
_____ copies of WWF Discussion Leaders Guide @ $5.95 ea $_____
KY residents add 6% tax $ _____
Postage and handling $_____

TOTAL AMOUNT ENCLOSED $ _____

PLEASE ALLOW 2-3 WEEKS FOR US DELIVERY, CANADA 3-6